Patron-Driven Acquisitions

# Current Topics
# in Library and Information Practice

De Gruyter Saur

# Patron-Driven Acquisitions

## History and Best Practices

Edited by
David A. Swords

De Gruyter Saur

ISBN 978-3-11-025301-6
e-ISBN 978-3-11-025303-0

*Library of Congress Cataloging-in-Publication Data*

Patron-driven acquisitions : history and best practices / edited by David A. Swords.
   p. cm. -- (Current topics in library and information practice)
Includes bibliographical references.
ISBN 978-3-11-025301-6 (acid-free paper) -- ISBN 978-3-11-025303-0 (e-book)
1. Patron-driven acquisitions (Libraries) 2. Academic libraries--Acquisitions.
3. Libraries and electronic publishing. I. Swords, David A.
Z689.P38 2011
025.2'3--dc23
                                 2011028127

*Bibliographic information published by the Deutsche Nationalbibliothek*
The Deutsche Nationalbibliothek lists this publication in the Deutsche
Nationalbibliografie; detailed bibliographic data are available in the Internet
at http://dnb.d-nb.de.

© 2011 Walter de Gruyter GmbH & Co. KG, Berlin/Boston

*Cover:* Photo by Alexander Swords

Typesetting: Dr. Rainer Ostermann, München
Printing: Hubert & Co. GmbH & Co. KG, Göttingen
∞ Printed on acid-free paper

Printed in Germany

www.degruyter.com

# Contents

Part 3 – Modeling PDA

Part 4 – Conclusion

# Acknowledgments

Above all, I thank the authors of the chapters that comprise this volume. Each one of them has a profoundly busy professional life, yet they somehow found time to write these chapters. And in my opinion, none of them did perfunctory work; they all have given us clear, original, informed thinking on the subject of PDA. It is also important to say that the appearance of their names in this volume does not mean they share my opinions or one another's opinions about PDA. One of the strengths of this book is that it gives the reader many windows into the developing world of PDA. Also I thank Mike Shatzkin for his generous willingness to talk about PDA, a subject with which he had no experience and lots of wisdom. Finally, thank you Alice Keller, editorial director of the Walter de Gruyter series in which this volume appears. She took the idea to her executives and persuaded them that the time had come for a book on PDA. She has been patient, wise, funny, and always a good friend.

# Editor's Note

Patron-driven acquisitions or acquisition (PDA), demand-driven acquisitions, patron-selection programs, user-driven collection, research-driven acquisition model, patron-initiated purchase, and their derivatives are synonyms in this book. Some authors prefer one term or the other and for defensible reasons. At this time, PDA seems likely to prevail in library parlance. It would not be my choice, given that "personal digital assistant" and "public display of affection" spoke for the letters quite awhile back.* And we cannot be sure that it will prevail. While the marketplace of ideas makes up its mind, for purposes of this book, whichever variation or variations an author has chosen stands.

---

\* A young friend told me recently that he has been "banned from the Denver Zoo for too much PDA." To squelch any rumors, the friend who said this was not Michael Levine-Clark.

# Introduction

## David Swords
*Ebook Library*

From the ancient library at Alexandria until the 1990s, libraries had been above all warehouses for books. They were orderly warehouses, but to be sure, they were warehouses. Perhaps it was the abrupt shift in journals from paper to electronic that began remaking libraries, but other important forces have been at work as well. One not to be over-looked was the transformation of bookshops, in the United Stated led mostly by Barnes & Noble, into spaces that looked like libraries, that had their *gravitas*, their dark wood, but that were deliberately commodious, that included coffee shops and comfortable chairs, that invited not just standing and browsing among the shelves but comfortable reading for hours. I remember being in Greenville, South Carolina, in the mid '90s where on any Saturday Barnes & Noble was the most popular nightspot in town, choked with people sprawled everywhere, drinking coffee, talking seriously, and reading. The Eighteenth-Century English coffee shop had come to the Twentieth-Century American bookstore.

Not long after, academic libraries began to follow the lead of their retail cousins. Where formidable librarians had forbidden food and especially drink, they included coffee shops of their own. Where they had been quiet as the cloistered monasteries of the Middle Ages, they became gathering places for students who used the library to meet and talk through, or even act out, assignments.

The evolution continues today as libraries wrestle, for example, less with the issue of which books to buy than with the more pressing issues of which books and how many to weed, so that they can open space formerly devoted unquestioningly to shelves, to other practices. Cushing Academy in Ashburnham, Massachusetts, whose Library Director Tom Corbett describes their evolution in Chapter 6 of this volume, scandalized Boston in fall 2009 when the school announced its intention to do away with its print collection. But far from the philistine practice for which Cushing was pilloried in the *Boston Globe*, the school had taken a bold step in recognizing that its library could serve the Cushing community far better by becoming something more like a media center, a gathering place where people can talk, can study television or radio as well as books and journals, can get to assignments online and on Blackboard, and can bring the outside world to them and go out to the world from the space the library has become. People have said to me down the years that students no longer go to their campus libraries, have no need to go to them when Google is everywhere, and especially in every Starbucks. But those people have not visited the libraries where I go, such as the Scott Library at York University in Toronto, where students and their ubiquitous backpacks sprawl through every inch of the new information commons. They have not seen the beautifully functional library at the American University of Sharjah in the United Arab Emirates, where students occupy media rooms on some floors and on others, spaces where cell phones are allowed or spaces where they are forbidden. They have not visited the renewed library at Ohio State University, which houses only a percentage of its old book collection in favor of spaces that invite learning in all its forms.

As we begin to examine the thinking of many of our best minds on what is being called patron-driven acquisitions (PDA), it is useful to understand the environment into which this practice comes. In some ways PDA is the child of research that shows library selectors, dedicated to building timeless and timely collections as they are, cannot predict which books people will use and which will languish unused on shelves for decades. PDA is equally a response to recession and diminished budgets, which have led both to the need to buy fewer books and to the need to repurpose staff to public service as positions are discontinued, even as the library becomes busier. And PDA is the child of academic administrators who have instinctively questioned the need for the immense, never-ending blackhole of materials budgets in the face of the need to terminate staff and to apply money to rebuilding and building essential infrastructure. PDA is the result of all of these forces.

But more than these PDA is the product of technology and very specifically of the coming of age of ebooks. Publishers, who have been the objects of ire for their adherence to old ways in the face of new technology, deserve credit for their willingness to go along with PDA as a method for libraries to acquire books. As Chapter 7 discusses, they have been and are wary of PDA, but enough have swallowed their fears and forged ahead that the practice can now be a main method of acquisition even in the largest ARLs (see Dennis Dillon's Chapter 10 on PDA at the University of Texas, Austin). What publishers have specifically allowed is libraries to put bibliographic records into their catalogues for books, and especially for ebooks, that they do not own. When searches discover these records, a url links patrons out to the books themselves, where the entire work can be browsed. Under some systems the browse period allows all patrons a window in which they can decide whether a book suits their needs before a transaction that costs the library money occurs. In the most economical approach to PDA, whose value Doug Way and Julie Garrison quantify in Chapter 9, when patrons need a book the library pays for a short-term loan, usually 5 percent to 15 percent of the list price, rather than paying full price for a volume that far too often under traditional acquisition methods, might never be used again. In short, PDA establishes a specific measured connection between the cost of material and its usefulness to the community of library patrons. Libraries pay full price for books that are used extensively, pay by the use for books that are used lightly, and pay nothing for books that simply dwell in their catalogues as unwatched bibliographic records.

Why are ebooks critical to this practice? First, they can be delivered instantly. Even if printed in the library through a print-on-demand machine, but more typically delivered from a warehouse hundreds of miles away, print cannot easily satisfy the spreading human demand for instantaneity. Second, ebooks take up no space. When Cushing Academy pitched its collection of some 25,000 books, it opened the library for uses besides warehousing. But it also replaced the print with an ebook collection of some 160,000 titles, which it obviously could never have physically housed. Third, space has specific costs. Rick Lugg (Chapter 1) estimates that on average libraries spend $4.26 per year keeping each book available on a shelf. With ebooks, all of that money can go to other purposes, including to making available to patrons a larger slice of the canon of books. Which leads, fourth, to what I believe to be the most important contribution of PDA to our research libraries. In Chapter 5, Rex Steiner describes how he has been able to use PDA to create a nearly instant collection with almost no money in his library in Azerbaijan, a task that for he and his co-author Ron Berry in the past has taken years and hundreds of thousands, even millions, of dollars. As I write this introduction, the Azerbaijan Diplomatic Academy has "turned on" an ebook collection of 170,000 volumes for its students and faculty, with more titles added each month. If those books had to be purchased before they could be used, if they had to be shipped to the city of Baku on the Caspian Sea in the Caucasus, if they had to be processed and shelved, the library could afford only a tiny fraction of them. Instead, as libraries in developed and undeveloped countries are finding, PDA has an exponential democratizing effect. Academies can afford to allow access to what they could never afford to buy. The libraries become much better resources, and if they wish can radically rethink their role and their identity. Most important, because the people who use them have more of the best that has been and is being thought and said at their command, those people can become better citizens of the world.

In conclusion, I should say that if this introduction has been mostly philosophical, it belies the purpose of this book, which is, in fact, mostly practical. As Kari Paulson points out in Chapter 4, PDA as we see it today had its origins in Australia among Australian librarians not long after the turn of the Century, and in that country is now an established acquisitions practice, not an experiment. While a relatively few libraries have full-blown programs elsewhere, the collective experience represented by authors of chapters in this book demonstrates that PDA can be predictably implemented and managed in libraries that serve large and small communities. Sue Polanka and Emilie Deliquié offer an assessment of the different approaches ebook aggregators take to PDA (Chapter 8), and Michael Levine-Clark describes how he has managed the issues that bringing up a PDA program in his library has required (Chapter 3). All of us who have worked on this book believe that PDA has valuable widespread application for secondary-school, college, and research libraries worldwide. That said, Bob Nardini sounds a cautious note in Chapter 2 that deserves to be heard.

My fellow authors would say that if called upon they will thoughtfully offer to any of you who take up this volume the benefit of their experience with PDA.

*David Swords, Warner, New Hampshire, 1 July 2011*

# Part 1
# Background and Reasons

# Chapter 1
# Collecting for the Moment:
# Patron-Driven Acquisitions as a Disruptive Technology

Rick Lugg
*R2 Consulting LLC*

In early 2011, as this is written, patron-driven acquisition (PDA) has become one of the most discussed ideas in the world of library collections. PDA has the potential to fundamentally transform decades of library practice, along with long-established relationships among publishers, book vendors, libraries, and library users. Like all game changers, the basic idea is simple. Instead of acquiring books that users *might* want, the library provides a broad range of new title information, enabling patrons to choose which books the library should buy. PDA also enables acquisition at the point a title is needed, rather than buying speculatively and holding in anticipation of use; "just-in-time" access replaces "just-in-case" collecting. In other words, PDA emphasizes collecting for and at the moment of need, to supplement or replace the more traditional philosophy of collecting for the ages. Several trends have converged to make this idea especially compelling right now.

## The Academic Library Environment

Let's begin with some background. First, over the past decade, academic libraries have undergone a rapid transition from print to electronic resources as the dominant information format. In most libraries, 65 to 70 percent of the materials budget is claimed by electronic journals, full-text databases, e-reference works, and increasingly electronic monographs. Licensed or purchased e-resources are augmented by many free online resources, and digital access to most current government documents. Streaming audio and video are increasingly common. In most libraries, full-text downloads outstrip print circulation rates by orders of magnitude. In short, digital resources are the default choice for users, and their share of the library budget is large and will continue to grow. The prevalence of e-resources has radically changed user expectations regarding availability and delivery of content. The array of full-text resources commonly available to users in 2011 dwarfs what was available even five years ago. Even in the smallest institutions, immediate remote access to tens of thousands of e-journal titles, full-text databases, and ebooks is expected – and routinely delivered by the library.

Second, recent economic events, triggered by the 2008 recession, have resulted in massive budget pressure for most libraries. Cuts to higher education and library operating budgets will extend to mater-ials budgets, which are likely to be smaller in the foreseeable future. Given the existing commitment to e-resources, most of which involve recurring expenditures, there will be still less money available for discretionary book purchasing, especially for print books. It is more important than ever that the right books – books that patrons will actually use – are bought with these limited funds. Nonetheless, although fewer print books may be purchased overall, new business models for chapter-level access, short-term rental, and print-on-demand could result in more parts of more books being used more often.

Third, many libraries face competing priorities for space. Decades of just-in-case collecting have resulted in library stacks filled to capacity but seldom visited. Simultaneously, library gate counts are rising, as students congregate in the library to study, work together, visit the writing center, and drink coffee. On most campuses, the library remains an important hub, irrespective of collection use. Information commons, teaching and learning centers, group study space, information fluency, and other programs are in high demand, and compete with the low-use stacks for space within the library. In the words of space planning expert Scott Bennett, "Library after library has sacrificed reader accommodations to the imperatives of shelving. The crowding out of readers by reading matter is one of the most common and disturbing ironies in library space planning" (Bennett 2003). The obvious solution is to manage print collections more intelligently, and to limit space for stacks to those print titles most likely to be used.

The idea of establishing a fixed "carrying capacity" for print collections flies in the face of years of library practice. It also requires action at both ends of the print lifecycle. To keep onsite collections within a desired footprint, the library will need to both reduce the flow of incoming tangible material and remove low-use titles from prime central campus space. These titles may go to remote storage or be discarded, preferably in coordination with consortial partners in a shared print archive. But some action must be taken. Otherwise, the library runs the risk of becoming (and becoming viewed as) a warehouse for unused books, rather than a vital part of teaching, learning, and research outcomes.

Fourth, the lifecycle costs associated with retention and management of print collections are high. In Paul Courant and Buzzy Nielsen's chapter "On the Cost of Keeping a Book," the authors estimated that each volume retained in open library stacks cost $4.26 per year (Courant 2010). Retention in high-density storage facilities reduces the cost per volume, but it remains significant. As the authors state in their conclusion, "it is important to recognize that the costs associated with a print-based world, often assumed to be small, are actually large" (Courant 2010). Many libraries are grappling with how to control these costs by participating in shared print storage programs or by adopting a more sustainable approach to print collections. While ebooks also have lifecycle management costs, they clearly do not have the same need for space; they do not "crowd out readers" as print books do. In fact, ebooks make more room for users.

Fifth, the rise of the Web has changed user expectations related to information seeking. In the self-service ethic of the Web, libraries have begun to emphasize getting their resources into *user* workflows – on meeting users where they work – rather than expecting users to come to the library building or website. Users are changing. Undergraduates regard the library building more as study space than as a source for information. Most library resources are used remotely and electronically. In a recent project at an ARL library, R2 Consulting (my company) encountered graphic evidence of this. In one year, this library circulated 426,937 items, including renewals. Even at this seemingly robust level, circulation had declined 45.9% between 2003 and 2009. In the same year, however, the library experienced 2,422,024 full-text downloads.

While one statistic favors books and the other articles, the 6:1 preference for remote electronic access over physical check-out is compelling. The library's busiest front door is clearly its virtual one. But contemporary students also expect that library resources and services will be pushed out to other environments in which they work. These include course management systems such as Blackboard and Moodle; subject or course-specific resource guides, such as LibGuides; and mobile applications, etc. The availability of content in digital form is essential to meeting users in this way. Convenience for the user predominates, and immediate access to user-prioritized content is a key element of attracting people who have other information-seeking options.

Sixth, use of print monographs has been low historically and continues to decline. In 1979, when Allen Kent and his colleagues at Pittsburgh published the results of their study of circulation at the University of Pittsburgh's Hillman Library, competition with e-resources was not a factor. Even then, "if a minimum of two uses were established as the minimum criterion, 71% of the titles [purchased in 1969], would never have been bought" (Bulick 1979). In November 2010, Cornell University Libraries reported that 55% of monographs the libraries owned published in 1990 or later had never circulated (Cornell University Task Force on Print Collection Usage 2010). This coincides very closely with anecdotal evidence from other libraries of all sizes. Perhaps of more concern is that a greater portion (64.5%) of books published in 2001 had not circulated by the end of 2009. And of still greater concern: on April 19, 2010, only 10.5% of books checked out from Cornell's libraries were in the hands of undergraduates (Cornell University Task Force on Print Collection Usage 2010). While we must be careful not to overreact to these findings, it is no longer justifiable to do nothing, considering lifecycle costs and the many higher-value uses to which central campus space could be put. The low circulation rate among undergraduates bears close watching and confirmation in other studies. If circulation proves to be markedly lower among these younger users, we will have a sobering picture of future print use.

The ability to measure use of electronic resources conveniently, through COUNTER-compliant statistics, link-resolver link-outs, and so forth, has heightened interest in measuring the use of print. Again from the Cornell report, "Usage data is regularly consulted for the electronic resources in which the Library invests but, up to now, such data has not been systematically examined in the case of print materials." Dating back to the Kent study, published in 1979 but focused on books purchased in 1969, librarians have been aware that use of print books is disturbingly low, despite concerted efforts to select the best titles. In the evolving culture of assessment in higher education, as libraries are being asked to demonstrate their value to research and learning outcomes, print collections represent a drastically under-utilized resource, with a correspondingly low return on investment (ROI). University administrators now expect libraries to act on this information.

Finally, better archiving arrangements make it more acceptable to rely on ebooks for delivery of content to users, without the need to retain a corresponding print copy. As of February 13, 2011, Hathi Trust (www.hathitrust.org) lists 4,484,513 book titles that have been digitized in full text and archived to preservation-level standards in a trusted digital repository. Approximately 25% of these have been published since 1990. Large publishers such as Elsevier and Springer have escrowed their content with national libraries for safekeeping in the event of business disruptions. Shared print archiving for monographs is developing rapidly, assuring that print copies are available for error correction and re-digitization if necessary. This reduces the need for individual libraries to acquire and retain print, and increases comfort with a "collecting-for-the-moment" model.

The convergence of these factors creates an unprecedented opportunity to rethink library collections and acquisitions practice. Patron-Driven Acquisition, especially when applied to ebooks, has the potetial to address all of these problems to some degree. It delivers monographs in electronic, remotely accessible form, the preferred alternative for many users. In some transaction models, PDA alleviates budget pressure by enabling short-term rental of content, or purchase only after x number of uses. It eliminates the temptation and the need to buy speculatively. Ebooks do not occupy shelf space and are not subject to the costs of print lifecycle management (though they do impose other costs, especially in the management of cataloguing, item, and holdings records.) PDA puts library resources conveniently into user workflows, especially when the library enables unmediated access to a title discovered in the catalogue by a user. Finally, titles selected through PDA are guaranteed at least one use, by the patron who requested the item. This ensures that investment in collections has a direct benefit to users. PDA for ebooks makes it possible to collect for the moment of need without bearing the full cost of collecting for the ages.

## PDA: A Disruptive Technology

The philosophical shift underlying PDA is profound and multi-dimensional. Instead of curating collections of tangible materials, libraries have begun to adopt a new role: curating a discovery environment for digital materials. Instead of deliberately trying to identify titles most relevant to curriculum and research interests within a discipline, broad categories of material that *may* be relevant are enhanced for optimum discoverability, immediate delivery, and partial or temporary use. Instead of purchasing materials just in case a scholar may one day need them, PDA offers "just in time" access to needed titles or portions of titles. Instead of collecting for the ages, libraries are using PDA to enable more targeted collecting for the moment.

Although PDA is now most closely associated with ebooks, its origins lie in print resource sharing. In some respects, early work with print PDA served as a proof of concept. Good libraries have always incorporated some form of patron-driven acquisition, in the form of inter-library loan, direct borrowing from consortial partners, or special orders to vendors. Good collections officers have always studied ILL requests to learn what users had to search elsewhere for, and have modified their selection practices accordingly (Ward 2003). Many libraries have implemented programs to purchase, rather than borrow, titles appearing in ILL borrowing requests. The University of Vermont embarked on a bold experiment with print-based PDA, relying on a rush-order arrangement with their vendor. All of these approaches enjoyed some success, improving service for users and saving money for the libraries.

But while it was a step in the right direction, print-based PDA ultimately proved too slow and awkward to stimulate widespread uptake. Supply chains for tangible material, even at their best, require days for delivery rather than hours or even seconds. Services such as RAPID drastically improved delivery times for articles by delivering a scanned copy electronically, further raising expectations for speed of fulfillment for material requested from other libraries. Although it is not yet practical to apply this technique to books, the increasing availability of current ebook titles, combined with innovative transaction models such as short-term circulation, neatly sidestep the print-related supply chain issues. Under the right circumstances, immediate access for users is possible. It is clear that ebooks (and perhaps POD, given mixed feelings about reading book-length text on screen) are much better suited to the patron-driven model than past options.

However, even though ebook PDA solves many problems for libraries and users, its arrival on the market is accompanied by a sense of unease. The convergence of electronic monographs and support for patron-driven transactions constitute a new product, one that exhibits many of the characteristics of a "disruptive technology," a concept introduced by Clayton M. Christensen in *The Innovator's Dilemma* (Christensen 2003). There are several elements of his definition that resonate fully with PDA, once the language has been adapted from the corporate world to an academic library context.

- **PDA brings to the library and library users a very different value proposition than had been available previously**. PDA differs from traditional purchasing of both print and ebooks, and brings new options to both libraries and users. Books no longer need to be purchased speculatively. Transactions other than purchase are supported, including short-term circulation, a specified number of uses before purchase, and automatic purchase. Acquisition can be mediated or unmediated, depending on the library's preference. Choice of resources is shifted toward the patron. Fulfillment is immediate from anywhere.

- **"Products based on disruptive technologies are typically cheaper, simpler, smaller, and frequently, more convenient to use."** PDA saves money by enabling more granular management of expenditures, and minimizing purchase of material that will remain unused by improving discoverability. It also saves money by offering access models other than outright purchase. A much broader array of titles is potentially available in a discovery environment with which users are already familiar. Access options blend into the user's discovery workflow. Catalogue records are supplemented by rich metadata and by the ability to browse full-text for a limited time. Rules-based use thresholds can trigger automatic or mediated access or purchase.

- **The library's most powerful stakeholders generally don't want, and indeed initially can't use, a product based on disruptive technology. Disruptive technologies are first adopted by "emerging" or "insignificant" stakeholders**. The library's stakeholders represent a more varied group than Christensen's "most profitable customers," but similarities exist. Those stakeholders include university or college administration (who fund the library); faculty, graduate students, and undergraduates (who use the library); and library staff (who operate the library). The most powerful of those groups are typically the funders, high-status users such as faculty, and, in a surprising number of cases, library staff members, who embody the library's values. These groups have well-established expectations, work habits and practices. They expect the library to own or obtain the resources that could be needed for their work. They "don't want, and indeed can't use" (or see the need for) a new approach. These groups are most likely to retain a traditional view of the library's role and to be most satisfied with continuous refinements to that approach.

In Christensen's formulation, disruptive technologies such as PDA are first and most readily adopted in "emerging" or "insignificant" markets. In the academic context, these markets are likely to be made up of students, and especially undergraduates. These users have little investment in the current model of resource acquisition and circulation. (Remember that in Cornell's recent circulation study only 10.67% of books in circulation on a given day were checked out to undergraduates, who represent by far the greatest number of potential users.) Contemporary undergraduates are digital natives, imbued with the Web culture of self-service, desktop or mobile access to digital content, and immediate availability. They are the "emerging" market, whose needs are most likely to be completely satisfied with this new approach.

## Disrupting the Supply Chain

While the specific effects of disruption caused by PDA – and more generally by ebooks – will take years to become fully apparent, it is already possible to detect some changes, both in the supply chain and in libraries themselves. PDA is disruptive in a literal sense, threatening to alter established relationships and practices in publishing, in library bookselling, and within libraries.

In a patron-driven world, academic publishers are likely to sell fewer copies of each new title at point of publication. If adopted at scale, PDA will eliminate a portion of the print monograph library market, long a mainstay for university presses and STM houses. Instead of 500 copies of a new title being automatically distributed to academic libraries, thousands of copies of cataloguing records will be distributed. These generate no revenue, and guarantee no sales; in effect, they become a new form of marketing, mediated by the library but aimed at end users. Because some PDA models enable rental or short-term circulation, it seems likely that fewer books will be purchased outright. Approval plans will be modified to deliver fewer books automatically, whether in print or electronic form. Speculative purchasing will diminish. At minimum, as ebook PDA becomes more widely adopted, the formerly stable library market will become much less predictable and reliable for publishers. It is not at all clear that existing publisher business models can adapt well to this altered environment.

On the other hand, PDA may open up sales for publishers in different ways. A greater number of titles will be added to library catalogues, increasing the chance of discovery, use, and revenue. Controlled browsing and full-text searching will help users find chapters or sections of books they may have missed under the traditional model. There is a higher likelihood of use and purchase, since the PDA approach puts content directly into user workflows. Micro-transactions such as rental and short-term circulation will create new revenue streams to offset reductions in old revenue streams. If given a chance, PDA might actually prove to be a more rational economic model for distribution of scholarly content. In the words of Steve Smith, a subject specialist at Wellesley College, "I have no program in Asian microeconomics and would never buy a book on the subject outright. But because of short-term loans I can put records for these books in the catalogue. And they get used, at a cost I can afford and in a way that makes the library better for our patrons." It is entirely possible that all will be well, and that sales may even improve for some publishers. But there will be a great deal of uncertainty, and the experimentation and patience required may outstrip the reserves of some publishers.

Print book vendors will also be affected. The consolidation of firms within the market has been driven by many factors, but chief among them are library budget pressures and coming to terms with ebooks, and now PDA. The predominant library suppliers for print (YBP, Coutts, Blackwell and Dawson for English-language; HARRASSOWITZ, Casalini, Puvill, Erasmus, Aux Amateur and EastView for European languages) are all developing or considering ebook offerings, sometimes on their own, but more often in partnership with ebook aggregators. As with publishers, sales of print monographs to libraries by vendors face inexorable decline, as speculative buying is replaced by patron-driven models and reliance on rich metadata and access on demand. Approval plans involving automatic shipment – the predominant form of speculative buying – will be especially hard hit as more titles become available for ebook PDA.

At the same time, print book vendors offer some competencies critical to an effective PDA service, such as the ability to profile books and libraries for relevance. Some PDA programs already rely on these highly evolved methodologies to shape the list of titles to be made available to a particular library's users. Monograph vendors can also provide expertise with creation and delivery of cataloguing records to support PDA. Their online transaction systems can assist with duplication control and format preferences during the long transition period when both print and electronic versions are routinely offered to libraries. To reach its full potential, PDA will require many of these competencies, in addition to those new competencies offered by ebook providers. The result, for the foreseeable future, will be "co-opetition" – an uncomfortable mixture of cooperation and competition – between ebook aggregators and print book vendors (and others) seeking to transform their services.

Ebook aggregators such as EBL, ebrary, NetLibrary, and MyiLibrary are the primary disruptors of the market, though publisher-direct offerings also play a role. The ebook vendors offer some of the most relevant content through new business models and delivery options. They have pioneered the transaction models that make PDA possible. These firms both collaborate and compete with the print suppliers. That collaboration is crucial during the transition, when libraries are still buying mostly print books, and when the number of new titles available as ebooks pales in comparison to the number available in print. This will change quickly, as the proportion of ebook to print book purchases shifts, and as more ebook titles become available simultaneously with (or in place of) print.

Partnerships and ownership arrangements among ebook vendors now extend to sellers of non-book content – for example, ProQuest's recent purchase of ebrary, and EBSCO's purchase of NetLibrary. It is interesting to note that both ProQuest and EBSCO also offer discovery-layer software (Summon and EDS, respectively). In short, the selling of ebooks to libraries will look radically different in five years. It is difficult to predict the particulars, but one can imagine the basic characteristics of a successful model. PDA offerings that prevail will be tightly integrated with new user discovery environments, offer flexible transaction models, and will enable a choice of immediate electronic access, optional purchase of a print or print-on-demand version. Both institutional and individual action will be possible; that is, in some instances the library will purchase or rent the content on behalf of a patron, and in others the patron will purchase or rent the content independently. PDA may also be somewhat fragmented, as large publishers continue to push proprietary solutions for their content, and force libraries and individuals to operate outside of aggregator offerings. In the interim, the relationships of all players in this market will be subject to the volatility that accompanies innovation and environmental change. The library book market is well and truly disrupted.

## Disrupting Library Practice

It is within libraries, however, that the potential disruption caused by PDA is greatest. PDA strikes at the heart of the academic library's role as a mediator between the body of published content and potential users of that content. By putting selection and purchasing power directly in the hands of users, one of the library's most important historical roles fundamentally changes. The expert mediation of collection development diminishes in favor of a "crowd-sourced" approach to acquiring some library resources. The approach is unsettling. It calls into question the very concept of library collections and the traditional purpose of the library. Direct selection replaces mediated selection; access (or potential ownership) replaces ownership; collecting for the ages is replaced by collecting for the moment.

Instead of shaping a collection and attempting to acquire the best titles, the library's mediation shifts toward curating a discovery environment and toward serving as a purchasing agent. The library shapes the universe of possible resources and funds their purchase, but no longer chooses individual titles. While this may appear to presage a loss of control over library resources and a loss of influence over users, it may in fact represent only a change in the *locus* of influence. Instead of controlling which resources are purchased, library activity moves further into the user's workflow, engaging them in the selection process, but also enhancing discovery, associating resources with courseware or subject pages, and meeting users where they are working.

PDA offers options to offset this profound change – new forms of mediation that the library can employ to add value to its virtual interactions with users. These include selection of the titles to be added to the catalogue/discovery layer; the library decides what universe will be presented. Other mediation options include setting and managing a budget dedicated to PDA, which imposes some shape and necessary limits. In some PDA systems, the library can set its own thresholds for browsing, number of uses before purchase, and invoke short-term circulation or pay-per-view models. Mediation of patron requests by library staff can be imposed, eliminating duplication of titles already held in other formats, inappropriate requests, and other noise.

All of these are useful, and help to create effective PDA programs. But the toolset is very different from the toolset traditionally available to collection managers and library administrators. PDA tools are directed toward building an environment in which patrons can select, rather than building a collection of resources from which patrons can draw. They enable the library to enter the user's information-seeking process at a much earlier stage, but also limit the specificity of the library's advice to users.

As we contemplate the magnitude of these changes for libraries and librarians, it may be useful to remind ourselves of the ways in which libraries will continue to perform key functions, even as PDA alters the environment. How might these core competencies change in response to the disruptive PDA ebook technology? What is the library's role in a scenario where patrons do much of the selection? How can libraries adapt to this new model for resource identification, book selection and information seeking? Let us consider five key functions where library expertise remains central to a viable PDA program: selection; payment and budget management; discovery; lending and access; and archiving.

**Selection:** Selection is the activity that defines the universe of resources available to library users. In the print world, expert selectors create approval plan profiles and scan new title announcements, reviews, and catalogues to choose books most relevant to the curriculum and research interests of the departments they support. Patron-driven acquisition changes that activity, at least for some segment of the bud-segment of the budget. Patrons gain more influence over what the library purchases, and selectors exercise an "arbiter" role on fewer titles. For most selectors, it will be difficult to cede these responsibilities to patrons. In part, this is owing to a fear that popular titles might displace titles of lasting value, especially if undergraduate users are given free rein. And in part it is natural reluctance to admit that a function once considered important is now less so.

But in many ways selection is as important in the PDA world as ever. PDA programs rely initially on determining which categories of titles will be made available. Selection operates here very much as it does with approval profiles. Selectors must define the rules which govern relevance of subjects and acceptability of non-subject character- istics. Although the rules may be looser when titles are not being shipped automatically, good rules are still needed. Further, policies must be established to define browse and use limits. These relate to the choice of PDA platform, vendor, and business model. After a vendor is selected, purchase triggers, use of short-term selection, and other attributes must be decided. Use must be monitored. A budget for PDA must be established and its relation to the overall budget clarified; that is, the balance of expert selection and patron-driven selection must be worked out. Over time, performance must be evaluated, and perhaps withdrawal decisions made for some records in the catalogue. And, as noted previously, there is a great need for collections expertise in the creation of the discovery layer, and in helping to shape subject-specific or course-specific resource guides. Like library services generally, selection skills will move toward users.

**Payment and Budget Management:** Books purchased by individuals are purchased directly for use by the user. Books in libraries are purchased on behalf of potential users by the library serving as an intermediary. These are very different scenarios. PDA is an odd hybrid of the two, where the user chooses, but the library pays. This is understandably a source of discomfort, but the library can apply its acquisitions expertise to manage the situation. Most basically, control of the purse strings allows the library to shape the PDA program. The library can and must set institutional limits on PDA by imposing budgetary and subject caps. Though most PDA vendors offer some assistance in this area, there remains much to learn about managing a PDA budget to last through an entire fiscal year. This can be difficult even with expert selectors, but the sheer unpredictability of a much larger 'selector' base ups the ante.

By virtue of being the payer, the library gets to decide what transaction models it will support: borrow, buy, license, or rent; perpetual access or annual fee; single user or multi-user access; online only or downloadable. The library also retains the ability to turn the PDA program on and off as its budget requires. In short, the fiscal and business model controls imposed by the library are critical to the viability of the PDA approach; good acquisitions practice may make the difference between a program that is sustainable and one that is not.

**Discovery**: Discovery is the goal of selection, the point at which a user finds what he or she is looking for. Even in a print world dominated by expert selection, the aim has been to ensure that appropriate titles are available and findable in response to a user search. In other words, selection is an essential part of creating and maintaining an effective discovery environment. In the PDA world, the "curation" of this discovery environment is more important than ever – in part because there will be so many more potential resources from which to choose, and in part because users may need more guidance to separate signal from noise.

The PDA discovery environment begins with the subject and non-subject profiles offered by the approval vendor, the PDA vendor, or both. These establish the broad outlines of the library's interest and are applied to the titles offered by the respective vendors. Once the universe of PDA ebooks has been defined, several discovery tools come into play. These include MARC records imported to the library's catalogue, access to the PDA vendor's own site and catalogue, and incorporation of metadata into the library's own discovery layer software. Full-text indexing, extended title metadata, and online browsing all improve the chances of a user finding a relevant title. Links to course management systems and LibGuides, created and maintained by subject librarians, can suggest the best and most appropriate titles in the context where they are most likely to be sought. The extent and variety of such discovery support depends to some degree on PDA platform characteristics, but also on a library's own discovery systems infrastructure and the creativity of the library's staff. But there is no doubt that libraries will continue to add significant value here.

**Lending and Access:** The original patron-driven transaction is a purchase. But of course libraries perform a unique function; they buy books in order to lend them. This lending has controls, loan periods that are specified and enforced, copyright and license terms that must be honored. Access is restricted to authorized library users, controlled by IP ranges or password-protected. Single user or multiple user permissions are enforced. Any access problems experienced by the user receive troubleshooting attention from library staff. All of these skills are still required, some of them much more frequently, in a PDA environment.

**Archiving:** Another core academic library value – and competency – is the commitment to preserving the intellectual and cultural record. Under the expert model, a selection decision implies a corresponding commitment to retain and preserve that content. If a title is valuable enough to have been selected, it is valuable enough to secure its perpetual accessibility. This is what is meant by collecting for the ages. And this is an area where great care must be taken as the profession begins to embrace "collecting for the moment."

To ensure access at the moment a book is wanted – and especially if the library does not own the item – archival commitments are needed. Those commitments may take the form of perpetual access arrangements offered by most ebook vendors. But it is important to note that those provisions exist largely because libraries have pushed so diligently for them. Education and advocacy for preservation and archiving are library contributions that are vital to ebook and PDA programs. But so too is action. Hathi Trust, a secure digital archive that grew out of concerns over the Google mass digitization project, represents the best of library work in this realm. A proposed network of shared print archives, led by the Western Regional Storage Trust, Re-CAP, and the Center for Research Libraries, will supplement Hathi with another layer of content security. Library values, well implemented, will ensure the integrity of our scholarly record.

## Conclusion: A Dynamic Balance

As a promising new technology and business model is introduced, it is always tempting to apply it broadly. This is especially true in the case of PDA, since it addresses so many problems in the academic library environment. Its adoption can begin to ease space problems immediately. It places content in user workflows. Turning selection over to users at scale will improve use rates. Lifecycle management costs are likely to be lower. ROI on collections may improve significantly. These are all attractive possibilities.

But there are dangers as well as benefits in listening to users, as pointed out by Anthony W. Ulwick in the *Harvard Business Review* (Ulwick 2002). To summarize his warnings:

- Users have a limited frame of reference
- Users focus on past and current experiences
- Users tend to offer incremental, rather than bold, suggestions
- Users are less familiar with the potential of future possibilities
- Innovation is the responsibility of staff

The best expert selection has always considered users in the context of the best works available in a given subject. Expert selectors understand the literature of a discipline, the curriculum and research interests of the departments they serve, and budget realities. They may have a better sense of which works will stand the test of time. Most importantly, good selectors know how to balance these factors as they make decisions on individual resources. Even as some selection is turned over to users, some should remain in the hands of experts.

PDA and expert selection are not opposed to one another. They exist on a spectrum, and can complement one another. Both techniques are useful in the right circumstance. Collection use is important, and some books are better than others. Academic libraries need and can accommodate both expert selection and user-driven selection. A reasonable starting point may be to allocate half of the book budget for each, but of course needs and interest will differ locally. Each library must find its preferred balance between collecting for the ages and collecting for the moment, but every library can benefit from both perspectives. Disruption does not necessarily lead to destruction.

# References

Bennett, Scott. *Libraries Designed for Learning.* Washington, DC: Council on Library and Information Resources, 2003.

Bulick, Stephen, William N. Sabor and Roger Flynn. "Circulation and In-House Use of Books." In *Use of Library Materials: The University of Pittsburgh Study*, by Allen Kent et al., 9-55. New York: Marcel Dekker, Inc., 1979.

Christensen, Clayton M. *The Innovator's Dilemma.* New York: Harper Business Essentials, 2003.

Cornell University Task Force on Print Collection Usage. *Report of the Collection Development Executive Committee Task Force on Print Collection Usage.* Ithaca: Cornell University Libraries, 2010.

Courant, Paul N. and Matthew "Buzzy" Nielsen. "On the Cost of Keeping a Book." In *The Idea of Order: Transforming Research Collections for 21st Century Scholarship*, 81-105. Washington, DC: Council on Library and Information Resources, 2010.

Ulwick, Anthony W. "The Limitations of Listening to Users." *Harvard Business Review*, January 2002.

Ward, Suzanne M, Tanner Wray, and Karl E. Debus-Lopez. "Collection Development Based on Patron Requests: Collaboration between Interlibrary Loan and Acquisitions." *Library Collections, Acquisitions, and Technical Services 27 (2003)*, 2003: 203-213.

# Chapter 2
# Approval Plans and Patron Selection: Two Infrastructures

Bob Nardini
*Coutts Information Services*

## Approval Plans: A New Infrastructure

Approval plans killed patron selection. That was several generations ago in the large academic libraries of North America, when the introduction of approval plans was one big thing librarians did to take away the responsibility and budgets for book selection from academic departments. Before that it had been a librarian's job to order and catalogue books, to loan them out, and to keep things running inside the building. But selection of most books was performed by those with the deepest subject knowledge, academics.

The result, librarians came to feel, too often was an "unbalanced" collection, a collection full of idiosyncratic choices meant for no better purpose than narrow personal need (Alan, ed. 2005).[1] Collections, too, were riddled with "gaps," when faculty members who were unsystematic or lackadaisical in their selection duties missed important books. Faculty were also un-attuned to the rhythms of a fiscal year, sometimes spending all their book money too soon, so that months then went by

---

1 From the 1980s until his death in 2006, probably the most influential voice among collections librarians in the United States was Ross Atkinson. A measure of change in collection development ideas about patron relationship to selection over those years until today is to read this excerpt from a 1989 article, where Atkinson wrote, "it would clearly be detrimental to assign any privilege or priority to any particular method or instance of use … It is for this reason also that the building of research library collections cannot be left to individual users, such as university faculty. In fact, the more knowledgeable the user group, the greater the need for the collection to be built by an outsider who is willing to approach the documentation on the subject as an abstraction."

when nothing at all could be bought; and at other times waiting until too late in the year, burdening librarians with having to spend budgets furiously in a year's final weeks – often at the risk of losing the money if not spent in time – with orders that could instead have been regularly portioned out across the academic calendar.

## The Birth of Approval Plans

These ideas took shape in the 1960s and early 1970s, years when universities were flush, academic libraries were in an expansive frame of mind, and many librarians were eager to professionalize what became known as "collection development." It was the faculty's job to teach and write; it's ours to build the collections they'll need; and we can do it better than they can. That argument eventually won the day, as the belief that faculty, or "patrons," knew best which books belonged in the library was abandoned by librarians. An important vehicle for this movement and for its arguments to get on the record was a series of four conferences on approval plans held between 1968, when the first convened in Kalamazoo, Michigan, and 1979, when the fourth opened in Milwaukee (Spyers-Duran 1969, Spyers-Doran 1970, Spyers-Doran 1972). Articles were written and books published to debate and document the underlying questions, questions that without a doubt were at the same time taken up in ten thousand meetings and phone calls; hallway, quadrangle, and office encounters; and over drinks or coffee off campus.

For a time there was so much money to spend on books that libraries had trouble spending all of it. Creating and tracking orders, receiving the resulting flood of books, then providing the cataloguing and labeling and stamping necessary to put them onto shelves, all added up to a job at or beyond the capacity of many academic libraries. The approval plan was one way around the problem. Thousands of pertinent books could be received on a regular schedule without the work of creating and maintaining orders. The Richard Abel Company, of Portland, Oregon, developed and marketed the approval plan, and then the accompanying technical services, beginning in the mid-1960s (Newlin 1975, O'Neill 1973, Abel 1995).[2] During the 1970s, approval plans became widespread

---

2    In a series of articles published in *Against the Grain*, Richard Abel is now in the course of presenting a history of his company. The first installment

in medium-to-large academic libraries. Later they became all but universal (Flood, ed. 1997).

## A New Efficiency, a New Balance

Part of the argument for approval plans was carried by acquisitions librarians, who cited the efficiencies of buying books this way. Another part of the argument came from collections librarians, who said that selections would be balanced across curriculum and research needs; budgets would be spent rationally; and that key books would less often be overlooked. Even so, in these earlier years collection-development librarians often had an uneasy relationship with approval plans. With book expertise now available in-house – their expertise – why was anyone other than a library selector selecting books on behalf of the library (Nardini 1993)?

Well into the 1980s and sometimes beyond, the result in many libraries was a broad and even comprehensive approval plan for university press books, books easy to define then as the necessary "core" of an academic library's mission. Some libraries, in addition, had smaller approval plans for trade and other publishers; but others did not, leaving those choices in the hands of their selectors. One important part of a collection development librarian's job was to pay weekly visits to the approval plan review shelf, usually housed in the acquisitions department, where the latest book receipts were arranged in subject order for their inspection. Special forms were kept nearby to record their decisions to keep or reject a book; to apply this fund or that; and to assign to one location or another, instructions then carried out by acquisitions staff. Another important job was to select books beyond the scope of approval plan shipments, selections often made with the help of paper bibliographic slips provided by the approval plan vendor. Acquisitions staff then placed firm orders against these selections.[3]

---

was, Richard Abel, "Papa Abel Remembers – The Tale of a Band of Booksellers," *Against the Grain* 19 (February 2007): 74-75; and the most recent was, Richard Abel, "Papa Abel Remembers – The Tale of a Band of Booksellers, Fascicle 12: What's Your Role? Executive or Staff?" *Against the Grain* 22 (December 2010-January 2011): 64-66.

3   In 1979 approval plan procedures were formalized in a book: Jennifer S. Cargill and Brian Alley, *Practical Approval Plan Management*, Phoenix: Oryx Press, 1979.

When the nation's economy stalled in the 1970s – bringing down the Richard Abel Company – some librarians raised new questions about the wisdom of relying on private companies for book selection, as well as about the arithmetic of uncertain book budgets being spent on a flow of books not entirely within the library's control. Was the approval plan sustainable in a fluctuating economy (Maddox 1976)?

While no study ever answered that question in any definitive way, none was needed. The approval plan idea proved itself sustainable simply by spreading to more and more academic libraries across the remainder of the seventies, the eighties, the nineties, and then into the next century. The approval plan had performed exactly as advertised: if anything, even better. As budgets ebbed and flowed across those years, vendors and libraries learned to work together to adjust approval plan structures so that whether times were good or times were lean, the approval plan was how most new books a library was able to buy were bought. The approval plan proved not only the most efficient means of handling a surge in the book budget, but also an effective way of handling a cut (Leonhardt 1988). As up-and-down became a kind of norm, for librarians with no choice other than to value flexibility as they managed their domains, approval plans were among their most reliable tools.

## The Response to Change

When librarians discovered that some academic publishers were routinely charging a price for their "library edition" clothbound books that was a multiple of the paperback price, vendors incorporated an optional "paperback preference" into their approval plan profiles (Courtney 2002). When librarians began to look at standing orders that had been both established and forgotten years ago, benign neglect seemed too casual an approach and many series earlier set up this way were instead folded into approval plans (Rouzer 1995). When cataloguing and processing backlogs due to staff cutbacks and other reasons drew the attention of library administrators, vendors asked to ship books "shelf-ready" learned how and then routinely complied (Fiegen and Bosch 1997). When the World Wide Web was still a curiosity to many people, book vendors had already developed early interfaces providing librarians with efficient online searching and ordering as well as instant access to views of approval plan activity (Heller and Lorenzen 1999).

All these innovations became routine during the 1990s, as the academic library environment began to change in ways that continue to unfold. The role of "bibliographer" established in the prior generation diminished, as mastery of subject matter was surpassed in value to library administrators by mastery of the new technicalities and new and quickly developing business arrangements of the online world. Approval plans started to routinely encompass books beyond the university presses, as resistance fell away on the part of selectors whose attention and whose time, in the mid-to-late decade, shifted away from print and toward electronic journals and other online resources. Managing these resources, even to gain understanding of them, was a job that required time and energy on the part of librarians who shortly before would have been devoting themselves to the selection or acquisition of books. The approval plan, no longer controversial, brought in new books and spent budgets with minimum effort. Approval plans had become a piece of academic library infrastructure, like OPACs and reference desks.

## The Internet

By the mid-1990s library users had caught up and were routinely accessing the Web, a paradigm-changing phenomenon if ever there was one. Students became oriented toward the Web and many public services librarians, who at the same time might be book selectors, saw their primary mission as to help patrons to gain a deeper understanding of what it was they were doing online, along with more fluency in doing it. These efforts in "bibliographic instruction," later "information literacy," took a great deal of time, in teaching and in the preparation for teaching, time that often came at the expense of book selection and visits to the approval review shelf.

How many books that might once have been read or at least opened now stayed put on library shelves because patrons were consulting – or merely surfing – the Web? No one had an answer to that question, but the larger answer was hard to miss. For many users, books were less important than they had been in the past. Ambitious librarians looking to advance their careers saw that book selection, the responsibility once won away from teaching faculty, was no longer a promising route. If the approval plan had not been operating as routinely as it did, so that to a point books were taken care of, someone might have had to invent it.

When Google discovered books things changed again. Why, if every book in the world, or close to it, would soon be available to everyone, or close to it, did book selection matter? Why, with everyone sharing one big collection, did the local collection matter? Difficult now as it is to recall how recent the news was, only in late 2005 did Google announce plans to digitize and make widely available the many millions of books housed by a group of leading research libraries. Whatever "collection development" meant at that point, it had been years since librarians said it meant expert book selection on the part of bibliographers carried on simultaneously by every academic library of any size, anywhere in North America.[4]

If selectors seldom visited the approval review shelf and teaching faculty never did; if the library removed the new-book shelf from its prominent public space in favor of a bank of computers or a café; if electronic resources became the starting point and often the end point too of student research; and if book circulation statistics for many libraries dropped sharply while one of the director's headaches was the space claimed floor by floor by stacks of seldom used books; the approval plan kept on going nonetheless, preserving as if in amber the values of an earlier generation of collection development librarians (Courant and Neilsen 2010).

Nor was this an entirely bad thing. If book use was down it had not disappeared by any means, and significant constituencies on every campus were sure to be heavy and regular book users. The faculty in many disciplines, after all, continued to write books, to assign them, and to keep them at the heart of their credentialing process. If books were not as central as they once had been they had not gone away, and an approval plan remained an efficient way to acquire lots of them. While it was hardly news that many of the new books seldom circulated, and perhaps never would, the "just-in-case" argument for building research collections gave way to the desire, at least, to acquire materials "just-in-

---

4   "Good collections will not be developed by cutting staff and automating the selection process....What is needed, instead, is to hire more expert collection development librarians, and let them *select*," was possibly the last major published statement along these lines. See William S. Monroe, "The Role of Selection in Collection Development: Past, Present, and Future", in *Collection Management for the 21ˢᵗ Century: A Handbook for Librarians*, ed. G.E. Gorman Ruth H. Miller (Westport, CT: Greenwood Press, 1997), 115.

time," as these phrases borrowed from the literature of business became staples, even clichés, of the library literature too.[5]

## The Approval Plan Continues On

Infrastructure is easy to run but hard to replace. Unlike the card catalogue, there was no OPAC waiting in the wings to succeed the approval plan, which could seem like an old city bridge: still maintained and in daily working order, heavily used in fact; under-inspected for years, perhaps no longer the safest possible avenue; but an established path with no clear alternative route. And if, like OPACs – a piece of infrastructure of similar age – approval plans might be bridges to nowhere, who had an idea bright enough to take them down?

One thing about approval plans was certain: they put a lot of books on the shelves of academic libraries. If UCLA, for example, which had been an early adopter of approval plans in the 1960s, held 7,653,382 volumes in 2000/01 according to the Association of Research Libraries, and by the 2005/06 edition of *ARL Statistics* reported 8,157,182, it was a sure bet that many of the 100,000 or so volumes added annually in between had been acquired through an approval plan.[6] During these years it was common for larger research libraries to spend well over $1,000,000 every year on books from their major approval plan vendor.

Why so many books? The question would once have been dismissed by librarians as beneath answering. It was simply their job to buy books as deeply as a library could afford, since scholars and students were sure to need books, and sure to need many of the ones they bought. "Collection building" was the job at hand, and librarians devoted far more of their time in that direction than in assessing the value of the collections they were building. During the 1980s the "Conspectus" method of assessing and comparing collections, a system first developed

---

5   A search of *EBSCO host* performed on March 4, 2011, for the terms "'just-in-time' AND libraries" in "All Text" for "Academic Journals" for "Publication Date" January 1995 to December 1995 returned 78 results; while the same search for the same months in 2000 returned 368; and for 2005, 585.

6   "ARL Statistics Tables 2000-01" and "ARL Statistics Tables 2005-06," Association of Research Libraries, accessed March 4, 2011, http://www. arl.org/stats/annualsurveys/ arlstats/statxls.shtml.

by the Research Libraries Group to measure collection strength through a system of "levels" defined mainly in terms of volume count in discrete subject areas, was a method widely used, if sometimes ridiculed (Atkinson 1986, Henige 1987). Eventually use of the Conspectus withered and the only common and routine way of evaluating a book collection was simply to report the overall volume count.

## The Twenty-first Century: Count Versus Use

As the Twentieth Century gave way to the Twenty-first, however, it was obvious that a count of printed books was too crude a measure to satisfy anyone in an era when "accountability" had become a byword for institutions of every type. University libraries received no bye and so new systems of assessing library effectiveness were developed.[7] With the focus shifted to "outputs" rather than "inputs" such as volume count, it did not take long for questions to be raised more frequently about levels of collection use than levels of collection intensity. As soon as circulation count mattered as much or more to administrators than volume count, the glory days of collection building were over.

The famous Kent study at the University of Pittsburgh had been mostly ignored in practice over the years of collection building, but in the era of accountability it started to get some respect (Kent 1979). In 2010, for example, two issues of the longstanding journal *Collection Management* were published as a combined single issue covering the theme, "Patron-Driven Acquisitions." The joint issue contained fourteen articles on different aspects of the topic, several of which cited "Kent," but all of which honored Kent's spirit, which was that circulation should be an important measure of the value of an academic library's book collection.[8] Again, a measure of the distance collection develop-

---

7   Bruce Thompson, "The Origins/Birth of LibQual+", LibQual+, accessed March 4, 2011, http://libqual.org/about/about_lq/birth_lq.

8   Citing Kent were: Judith M. Nixon, Robert S. Freeman, and Suzanne M. Ward, "Patron-Driven Acquisitions: An Introduction and Literature Review," *Collection Management* 35 (2010): 123; Judith M. Nixon and E. Stuart Saunders, "A Study of Circulation Statistics of Books on Demand: A Decade of Patron-Driven Collection Development, Part 3," *Collection Management* 35 (2010): 161; Leslie J. Reynolds, et al., "User-Driven Acquisitions: Allowing Patron Requests to Drive Collection Development in an Academic Library,"

ment has traveled is to contrast the criterion of circulation with earlier ideas. The University of Wisconsin-Milwaukee's Richard Loreck was an attendee at the first national approval plan conference: "We operate on the principle or on the premise that we would rather have a book in the library and apologize for its being there than to defend the position of why we don't have a book. . . . To wait for a faculty member or a staff member to order a current title is a little too indefinite in our situation" (Loreck 1968).

That was then. Today it would be extremely difficult to find an academic librarian who would say anything like this. Instead, today's librarians are more likely to emphasize their relatively newfound capacity, on behalf of all campus users, not just "a faculty member or a staff member," to provide access to a bibliographic universe much wider than Richard Loreck and his colleagues could have imagined. Today it is not difficult to envision a bibliographic universe comprising mainly ebooks, titles that a library would not pay for until it reached a defined level of actual use made possible through bibliographic surrogates offered to a user community. Why pay for books that might never be used? How can any other way of assembling library collections be justified in today's economic and technological environment? Have academic libraries found a new infrastructure? In our own era, four decades after Richard Loreck, these same questions might be asked differently: Will patron selection kill approval plans?

## Patron-Driven Acquisitions: A New Infrastructure?

Approval plans may indeed outlive their usefulness – as soon as the day comes when all new books are immediately and always available for purchase or access as ebooks. Maybe that day is closer than any of us know, thanks to Google, or to some other agent as yet undreamed of, as Google was just a short time ago. In the meantime, however, in the midst of a much larger public discourse about ebooks than about print books, academic librarians will have to shape their book collections in the world they know, not in a world they can imagine. In today's world,

---

Collection Management 35 (2010): 254; David C. Tyler, et al., "Just How Right Are the Customers? An Analysis of the Relative Performance of Patron-Initiated Interlibrary Loan Monograph Purchases," Collection Management 35 (2010): 177.

and in the near future or likely longer, print still matters for academic libraries.

What have been some of the simplest routines in library acquisitions remain ebook question marks. To begin with, it is not easy today to know if a given title will be available as an ebook on a platform suitable for academic libraries. In fact most new titles offered by academic book vendors, let alone older titles, are not available as ebooks, and availability patterns by subject and publisher are anything but consistent (Price and MacDonald 2008). For those ebooks that do become available, the relative availability dates of the two formats are another question, today often resolved by a purchase of the known print book, not by a delayed decision hinging on the potential appearance of an ebook.

Why buy the "known" book, though? After all, while ebook availability may be far from universal there are plenty of them today, enough to provide content in most subject areas and so to meet the purpose of many students, which is simply to find some book material pertinent to an assignment. Does it make a difference which book they find, so long as they find one? Of course it often will make a difference to students in advanced classes and certainly will to the graduate students who need to immerse themselves in particular books. True enough, adequate library service in many undergraduate contexts could mean to have "some" material available, which could mean relying on ebooks and so on patron-driven acquisitions. One wonders though at what point it might be unwise, for the benefit of the more curious among these students as well as for the sake of opinion around campus of the library, to write off a significant number of available and often noteworthy books because of a preferred acquisitions method.[9] If a library's collection strategy is centered on ebook patron-driven acquisitions, for today, at least, it would

---

9    For example, a search on March 19, 2011, of two academic ebook platforms, ebrary and MyiLibrary, for 2009 National Book Award adult titles found two of the fifteen finalists available on both platforms, one available on one platform, and twelve available on neither platform. The three available books all were from university presses – California, Princeton, and Wesleyan – while ten of the twelve unavailable titles were from major trade publishers such as Random House, Knopf, and Norton, and two were from university presses, Wayne State and Pittsburgh. These findings provide a micro-example illustrating a larger pattern for today's academic ebook platforms: spotty coverage of university press titles and scarce coverage of trade titles.

seem wise to complement this arrangement with an arrangement for acquiring print.

To the degree, once more, that particular titles matter, how sure is it that any given ebook will in fact be perpetually available for purchase or patron access? Is it possible that publishers and aggregators will in time purge their servers of titles that have not sold well, putting some titles into what amounts to a kind of "out-of-print" status? Will academic publishers whose business model for monographs has depended on library-based selection and acquisition permit these ebook titles to be placed on patron-driven acquisitions programs? If the dwindling sales that remain in this market are made dependent on use, how many monographs will be published at all, and what will this mean to scholarship as we know it? When will ebook inter-library loan and ebook preservation be sufficiently developed so that questions about perpetual availability are effectively answered? Of course, due to today's robust out-of-print market and the emergence of print-on-demand as an attractive model for publishers, for most titles print availability of one kind or another seems all but certain. It is not difficult to imagine a world where print has become a backup or supplementary format to ebooks.

To return again to the present, however, print is not a backup book format. Even when both formats are available many academic users still favor print, a predilection likely to continue into the near future at least. Their disciplines might traditionally be print-oriented or might rely on illustrations that for technical and legal reasons are still problematic for ebooks; or in any discipline users, depending upon their immediate purpose, might favor a mix of print books and ebooks, perhaps using both frequently (Abbott 2008). Students too, in findings that may surprise, often favor printed books.[10] Book/diskette combinations, a longtime staple in many applied fields, are an ironic case where physical publication has so far proven a superior medium for this online form, since

---

10   "A Cover to Cover Solution: How Open Textbooks are the Path to Textbook Affordability," The Student PIRGs, accessed March 4, 2011, http://www.studentpirgs.org/textbooks-reports/a-cover-to-cover-solution; "BISG Survey Finds Students Prefer Print," *Publishers Weekly,* January 7, 2011, accessed March 4, 2011, http://www.publishersweekly.com/pw/by-topic/industry-news/publisher-news/article/45699-bisg-survey-finds-students-prefer-print.html; "JISC national e-books observatory project: Key findings and recommendations, Final Report," November 2009, accessed March 4, 2011, http://www.jiscebooksproject.org/reports/finalreport.

ebooks often do not accommodate the information on the diskettes so conveniently tucked into the back covers of their print vehicles. A recent literature review described "a complex and somewhat contradictory landscape of attitudes and opinions" about ebooks where "several studies have indicated generally positive views of electronic books," while "many reflect mixed or quite negative user responses" (Shrimplin, et al. 2011).

While the future of approval plans will principally depend on the ascendancy and acceptance of ebooks, approval plans will also be compared to other ways of acquiring print books. Some vendors offer patron-selection programs for print. To start an ebook-based program, all a library needs are bibliographic records and a business agreement. Print-based programs, with the same two prerequisites, require also that an interface be developed so that patrons can identify themselves at the point of their purchase request, enabling the library to know whom to notify when the book arrives. The time to fill a patron's request is another factor separating ebook-based programs, where access is instant, from print-based programs. A print-based program must have an internal mechanism either to forward a purchase request to the acquisitions department, for staff to find the supplier most likely to fill an order with dispatch, or to save staff time by simply forwarding an order to the library's primary book vendor and hoping for the best.

No matter how orders are placed, print-based patron programs will lack other constant advantages of ebook programs. A print book will require shelf space and an ebook will not. Any substantial print-based patron program will remind all acquisitions librarians that one reason approval plans grew in the first place was that they consolidated a large number of small transactions into a small number of large transactions and while at it, regularized spending and shipments across an entire year. Today, how many long-since-downsized acquisitions departments would be equipped to open and receive thousands of small packages resulting from thousands of patron selections which ebbed and flowed less predictably? How many library administrators would be willing to delay delivery of these patron requests because the acquisitions department asked suppliers to, "hold the books for a little while please," in order to consolidate shipments and smooth things out? For all these reasons, print approval plans, even though no checkouts are guaranteed for the books shipped, have not been seriously challenged to date by print-based patron programs. Ebook programs remain by far the most common patron-based approach. As Michael Levine-Clark of the

University of Denver wrote in the *Collection Management* special issue, "Because selection of e-books can trigger an immediate and seamless purchase, unnoticed by the user, e-books are the perfect medium for demand-driven acquisition" (Levine-Clark 2010).

## Future Infrastructures

It does not take much of a crystal ball to forecast that ebooks will continue to gain on print books – and not only in the public discourse. That, in turn, makes it easy to predict that patron-driven acquisition programs will continue to grow in academic libraries. The book you are reading is itself good evidence for that. Do these forecasts, however, necessarily lead to another, that approval plans will diminish and even disappear?

So far, approval plans have been able to adapt to the rise both of ebooks and of patron-driven acquisitions programs. For larger vendors, at least, the application of a "profile" to newly available ebooks, by subject, publisher, and other parameters – a profile that would seem familiar to Richard Loreck – is a core service. Some vendors can accommodate a timing difference between print editions and their ebook counterparts, so that an approval plan preference for ebooks by a selector is not routinely trumped by the earlier appearance of a print edition. Some vendors can accommodate the "approval" element in an approval plan for ebooks. That is, selectors can say "yes" or "no" to each ebook (or print title) in the vendor interface before invoicing, a new online form of the "approval review shelf" maintained in the physical world for so many years by acquisitions departments across North America.

Approval plan profiles are already an essential piece of patron-driven programs as well. One problem with the earliest programs was that bibliographic records were made available with little or no screening, resulting in the acquisition of titles more suited to patrons' non-academic pursuits than to anything having to do with their coursework or research (Price and McDonald 2009). Now, however, libraries normally seed new programs with a batch of selection records a vendor provides by retrospectively applying a "profile" to its database, so that titles unsuitable by subject matter, intended readership, or otherwise can be screened out. Some vendors can also provide an ongoing supply of new patron-selection records by means of ongoing application of a library profile to new titles. In effect, patron-selection records become a new kind of "slip," always a basic element of approval plans for library selectors. Now, something like an approval plan slip, but in the form of a bibliographic record in the library catalogue, presents itself to library patrons.

## Patron Selectors

How well will patrons acquit themselves as selectors? Will they prove better selectors than librarians or vendors? The evidence we have seems to say that patrons are the better selectors in at least one sense. Books chosen by users circulate more reliably than books selected in a traditional way (Price and McDonald 2009). In the long run, though, over years, what will the evidence look like? Will patrons continue to hold the lead, or will the data even out and their selections come to seem narrow, as they once did to librarians present at the birth of "collection development"? Is a count of print circulation or online access the only valid measure of use in the first place?

It is the easiest measure, one that assumes all uses to be equal in value. Of course anybody who has ever borrowed or used books from a library knows, in their own case, that this is not true. Is a single checkout of a monograph over an entire semester by a graduate student writing a dissertation equal to a brief checkout of a book that on inspection turns out not to be needed? If a senior scholar checks out a book not used for twenty years and it informs their next monograph, how does that count? If we can predict that a specialized monograph is likely to see no use for long stretches of time, but if used is likely to contribute to someone's scholarship, and can also predict that a topical, less specialized book will be used more frequently, how should we interpret and use these forecasts?[11]

More at issue, however, are the books that do not circulate, and we know that a significant percentage of new books never circulate for many years. Probably the most significant recent study of approval plans was published in 2010, based on research conducted at the University of Illinois at Urbana-Champaign and Pennsylvania State

---

11   An interesting use study in reverse might be to start with the results of use, not use itself, by looking at the book references in a noteworthy monograph, calculating how often they had been borrowed before our monograph's publication.

University, where Robert Alan, Tina E. Chrzastowski, Lisa German, and Lynn Wiley looked at circulation in these two libraries for books received on approval plans during their 2004/05 fiscal years. The authors found that by March 2007, about 70 percent of Penn State's approval books had circulated, while UIUC saw a rate of 60 percent. That of course meant that 30 percent and 40 percent, respectively, of the libraries' receipts had remained on the shelf. The authors took note of the "relatively high noncirculation rate," while remarking that "it is no longer economically feasible for large research libraries to acquire a certain percentage of books 'just in case' a title might be needed in the future" (Alan et al. 2010).

One interesting thing about the UIUC-Penn State study, though, was what it did not say. In their conclusion the authors asked if large approval plans were still "viable," if they were "outmoded," if "other collection priorities" should be supported instead (Alan et al. 2010). The authors called for better ways of gathering data on approval plans, for better ways of refining profiles, for better communication with vendors, and for new studies over time and across different libraries. They did not, though, mention any alternatives to the approval plan. The authors' hope seemed to be for better approval plans.[12]

## Better Approval Plans

Approval plan vendors ought to share that hope, and more than that ought to be doing something about it. Bringing ebooks into approval plans was a good start. Offering broader coverage of ebooks and better control of ebook and print availability should be areas of further focus. Introducing new approval plan parameters that suit the present century and not the past one – such as print-on-demand status, so that a purchase could be safely deferred because of ensured availability – would be smart. Another area for work would be better tools for consortia or other libraries who wish to collaborate on approval plans, perhaps to ensure that certain titles will be available somewhere within a group. And yet another would be closer coordination with patron-selection

---

12  For a recent outright endorsement of approval plans see, Arlene Moore Sievers-Hill, "Building Library Collections in the 21st Century – How Goes the Book Approval Plan in the Days of the eBook?" *Against the Grain* 22 (December 2010-January 2011): 73.

programs, including operational improvements, better management reporting, and customized profiles and online interfaces developed for interested scholars, or "patrons," to review new titles.

Approval vendors should also pay attention to what the UIUC-Penn State study said about non-circulation rates. They should work with libraries to find ways to identify profile parameters corresponding to likely use and then use circulation statistics to support or reject their hypotheses. An example would be for approval profiles to make better use of author background and reputation – for users with any knowledge of a field usually the most important thing in deciding whether or not to open a given book, but for approval vendors, an under-used bibliographic element. The frequently mentioned but poorly defined "core titles" idea, an argument from the start in favor of approval plans, could be a power-ful reason to continue them (Nardini and Getchell 1996). A broadening of vendor coverage into optional offerings for titles in non-core areas, bringing traditional approval plan efficiencies to a wider bibliographic universe would be useful, since without a doubt, research collections require far greater breadth than the ebook universe has been able to deliver to date. Other examples might include more titles from smaller publishers – those least likely to offer ebooks – and more titles in non-book formats.

Even with all of this, there seems little doubt that patron programs will grow larger, while approval plans will grow smaller. They have already, as book budgets stagnated while publisher and aggregator ebook packages eat into what used to be prime approval coverage areas. Approval plans in their beginning years displaced not only faculty selection but also publisher standing orders, at one time common but by the 1990s largely defunct as a way for academic libraries to buy books. Over the past decade or so the re-emergence of book publishers as direct sellers to academic libraries is a salient change in this market-place.

## Direct Sales from Publishers Re-emerge

Now the largest academic publishers are pressuring not only approval plans, but patron-driven acquisition programs as well. Today publishers like Springer, Elsevier, John Wiley, Brill, Oxford University Press, Cambridge University Press, and others have their own well-developed ebook programs that include packages, title-by-title buying, and even plans for patron-driven programs. Some want to offer their own patron-driven acquisitions programs.[13]

Several different groups and organizations are now attempting to organize ebook programs for smaller (which is not to say small) university presses. And two major ebook platforms – NetLibrary and ebrary – have recently been acquired by companies not used to title-by-title selling. EBSCO and ProQuest now have the chance to develop whatever business models they might like to try out on their new properties. In short, vendors who offer approval plans or patron-driven acquisitions programs are not the only contenders for the future of the academic library book market.[14] While a continued hybrid approach seems likely for academic libraries for a considerable time – an approach incorporating print books and ebooks, packages, subscriptions, patron selection, title-by-title buying, and approval plans too – the balance among these services, not to mention the names of the companies and organizations providing them, is less certain.

---

13   For example, Siobhan O'Leary, "Germany's De Gruyter Tests PDA ... Patron Driven Acquisition, That Is," *Publishing Perspectives*, March 11, 2011, accessed March 19, 2011, http://publishingperspectives.com/2011/03/german-publisher-tests-pda-patron-driven-acquisition-that-is/.

14   "E-Books Coming to Project MUSE," Project Muse, accessed March 4, 2011, http:// muse.jhu.edu/; "JSTOR Adds E-Books to Its Portfolio," *The Chronicle of Higher Education,* January 8, 2011, accessed March 4, 2011, http://chronicle.com/blogs/ticker/jstor-adds-e-books-to-its-portfolio/29576; "A University Press Ebook Consortium," April 30, 2010, Association of Research Libraries, accessed March 4, 2011, http://www. arl.org/bm~doc/mm10sp-maikowski.pdf; Norman Older, "Focusing on WorldCat, OCLC Sells NetLibrary to EBSCO, Thins FirstSearch," *Library Journal*, March 17, 2010, accessed March 4, 2011, http://www.libraryjournal.com/lj/technology productsvendors/884426-296/focusing_on_worldcat_oclc_sells.html.csp; Sean Fitzpatrick, "ProQuest Acquires ebrary," *American Libraries*, January 8, 2011, accessed March 4, 2011, http://americanlibrariesmagazine.org/news/01082011/proquest-acquires-ebrary; Clifford Lynch, "Imagining a University Press System to Support Scholarship in the Digital Age," *the journal of electronic publishing*, Fall 2010, accessed March 4, 2011, http://quod. lib.umich.edu/cgi/t/text/text-idx?c=jep;view=text;rgn=main;idno=3336451. 0013.207.

## The Fate of Approval Vendors

Perhaps the biggest challenge for approval plans will be for the vendors who offer them to make a convincing case to customers that libraries have long counted on their "approval plan vendors" for a good deal more than running approval plans. In their Web interfaces, duplication control measures, workflow consulting, technical services, retrospective collection development, not to mention in the approval plans themselves, vendors create and maintain a complex infrastructure, and often do so at no charge. This is an infrastructure that has enabled academic librarians to identify and acquire books efficiently enough that they have also directed time and attention toward a long list of other patron services.

The demise of Blackwell in North America might raise questions about what has been the industry's economic model, one little changed since the Richard Abel Company became the first of many companies to fail in what is not an easy business, and whether a different model, one where less of this infrastructure would be delivered without charge, is worth the services it might sustain. The setup and maintenance of a patron-driven acquisitions program, for example, is not only a complex – and so, expensive – vendor project in itself, but also an enterprise built with the very object of delaying sales that have been reliably made by approval plans upon a book's publication. At the very least, book vendors will need to look carefully at their own approval plan and associated operations, to make certain they are economically viable.

The economic model for vendors will be one variable in the approval plan's future. Others will be the pace of new title availability on academic ebook platforms, greater acceptance of ebooks by pa-trons, and cooperation on the part of publishers. These questions are partially out of the vendors' hands, but perhaps the most important question is not. If today's book vendors listen to librarians like those at UIUC and Penn State, as vendors have done in the past in times of changing circumstance, in the end Peter Spyers-Duran, an organizer of all four of the early approval plan conferences, may turn out to have been correct in 1968 to predict, "Approval plans are here to stay" (Spyers-Duran 1969).

## References

Abbott, Andrew. "The Traditional Future: A Computational Theory of Library Research." *College & Research Libraries* 69 (2008): 542.

Abel, Richard. "The Origin of the Library Approval Plan." *Publishing Research Quarterly* 11 (1995): 46-56.

Alan, Robert, et al. "Approval Plan Profile Assessment in Two Large ARL Libraries." *Library Resources and Technical Services* 54 (2010): 70, 74, 75.

Atkinson, Ross. "The Language of the Levels: Reflections on the Communication of Collection Development Policy." *College & Research Libraries* 47 (1986): 140-149.

Atkinson, Ross. "The Role of Abstraction in Bibliography and Collection Development," in *Community, Collaboration, and Collections: The Writings of Ross Atkinson*, ed. Robert Alan and Bonnie MacEwan. Chicago: Association for Library Collections and Technical Services, 2005: 236.

Courant, Paul N. and Matthew "Buzzy" Neilsen. "On the Cost of Keeping a Book," in *The Idea of Order: Transforming Research Collections for 21ˢᵗ Century Scholarship*, CLIR Publication no. 147. Washington: Council on Library and Information Resources, 2010: 81-105.

Courtney, Dana. "The Cloth-Paper Conundrum: The Economics of Simultaneous Publication." *Journal of Scholarly Publishing* 33 (2002): 202-229.

*Evolution and Status of Approval Plans.* SPEC Kit 221. Washington: Association of Research Libraries, 1997.

Fiegen, Ann and Stephen Bosch. "Vendor Preprocessing of Approval Material and Cataloging Records for the University of Arizona Library," in *Outsourcing Library Technical Services Operations: Practices in Academic, Public, and Special Libraries*, ed. Karen A. Wilson and Marylou Colver. Chicago: American Library Association, 1997: 15-27.

Flood, Susan, ed. *Approval Plans in ARL Libraries.* SPEC Kit 83. Washington: Association of Research Libraries, 1982

Heller, Anne and Elizabeth Lorenzen. "Online Ordering: Making Its Mark," *Library Journal* 124 (September 1, 1999): 153-158.

Henige, David. "Epistemological Dead End and Ergonomic Disaster? The North American Collections Inventory Project." *Journal of Academic Librarianship* 13 (1987): 209-213

Kent, Allen, et al. *Use of Library Materials: The University of Pittsburgh Study.* New York: M. Dekker, 1979.

Leonhardt, Thomas W. "The Importance of Approval Plans When Budgets are Lean," in *Acquisitions, Budgets and Material Costs: Issues and Approaches*, ed. Sul H. Lee. Supplement no. 2 to *Journal of Library Administration*. Binghamton, NY: Haworth, 1988: 1-13.

Levine-Clark, Michael. "Developing a Multiformat Demand-Driven Acquisition Model." *Collection Management* 35 (2010): 203.

Loreck, Richard. "Approval Plans Can Be Successful," in *Approval and Gathering Plans in Academic Libraries, 5. 1968.*

Maddox, Jane. "On My Mind ... Approval Plans – Viable?" *Journal of Academic Librarianship* 1 (1976): 22.

Monroe, William S. "The Role of Selection in Collection Development: Past, Present, and Future," in *Collection Management for the 21ˢᵗ Century: A Handbook for Librarians*, ed. G.E. Gorman and Ruth H. Miller. Westport, CT: Greenwood Press, 1997: 115.

Nardini, Bob. "Blackwell's." *Against the Grain* 21 (December 2009-January 2010): 73-74.

Nardini, Robert F. "Approval Plans: Politics and Performance." *College and Research Libraries* 54 (1993): 417-425.

Nardini, Robert F., Charles M. Getchell, Jr., and Thomas E. Cheever. "Approval Plan Overlap: A Study of Four Libraries." *The Acquisitions Librarian* 16 (1996): 93-95.

Newlin, Lyman. "The Rise and Fall of Richard Abel and Co., Inc." *Scholarly Publishing* 7 (1975): 55-61.

Nixon, Judith M., Robert S. Freeman, and Suzanne M. Ward. "Patron-Driven Acquisitions: An Introduction and Literature Review." *Collection Management* 35 (2010): 123.

Nixon, Judith M. and E. Stuart Saunders. "A Study of Circulation Statistics of Books on Demand: A Decade of Patron-Driven Collection Development, Part 3." *Collection Management* 35 (2010): 161.

O'Neill, Ann L. "How the Richard Abel Co., Inc., Changed the Way We Work." *Library Acquisitions: Practice & Theory* 17 (1993): 41-46.

Price, Jason and John McDonald. "Beguiled by Bananas: A retrospective study of the usage & breadth of patron vs. librarian acquired book collections." Claremont Colleges Digital Library, 2009, accessed March 4, 2011.

Price, Jason and John McDonald. "To Supersede or Supplement? Profiling E-book Aggregator Collections vs. Our Print Collections." 2008, Claremont Colleges Digital Library, accessed March 4, 2011, http://ccdl.libraries.claremont.edu/cdm4/item_viewer.php?CISOROOT=/lea&CISOPTR=161&CISOBOX=1&REC=1.

Reynolds, Leslie J., et al. "User-Driven Acquisitions: Allowing Patron Requests to Drive Collection Development in an Academic Library." *Collection Management* 35 (2010): 254.

Rouzer, Steven M. "Acquiring Monographic Series by Approval Plan: Is the Standing Order Obsolescent?" *Library Acquisitions: Practice & Theory* 19 (1995): 395-401.

Sievers-Hill, Arlene Moore. "Building Library Collections in the 21ˢᵗ Century – How Goes the Book Approval Plan in the Days of the eBook?" *Against the Grain* 22 (December 2010-January 2011): 73.

Shrimplin, Aaron K., et al. "Contradictions and Consensus – Clusters of Opinions on E-Books." *College & Research Libraries* 72 (2011): 182.

Spyers-Duran, Peter, ed. *Approval and Gathering Plans in Academic Libraries.* Littleton, CO: Libraries Unlimited, 1969.

Spyers-Duran, Peter and Daniel Gore, eds. *Advances in Understanding Approval and Gathering Plans in Academic Libraries*. Kalamazoo: Western Michigan University, 1970.

Spyers-Duran, Peter and Daniel Gore, eds. *Economics of Approval Plans*. Westport, CT: Greenwood Press, 1972.

Spyers-Duran, Peter and Thomas Mann, Jr., eds. *Shaping Library Collections for the 1980s*. Phoenix: Oryx Press, 1980.

Thompson, Bruce. "The Origins/Birth of LibQual+", LibQual+, accessed March 4, 2011, http://libqual.org/about/about_lq/birth_lq.

Tyler, David C. et al. "Just How Right Are the Customers? An Analysis of the Relative Performance of Patron-Initiated Interlibrary Loan Monograph Purchases." *Collection Management* 35 (2010): 177.

# Chapter 3
# Building a Demand-Driven Collection:
# The University of Denver Experience

Michael Levine-Clark
*University of Denver*

Academic libraries choose books to add to their collections based on many criteria including a judgment of quality, suitability for current curricula and faculty research needs, potential for use by future research-ers, price, and the amount of material on that topic already in the collection. To make these decisions, libraries have traditionally acquired books as close as possible to the date of publication. Doing so made sense for many reasons, most significantly because this might be the only chance to buy a book that would soon go out of print, but also because tools and strategies for discovery of books were based upon a physical book being on a physical shelf. Ebooks, new discovery tools, and changing publishing models make it possible for libraries to push the point of purchase to the point of need, and by so doing to build stronger and deeper collections.

The Penrose Library at the University of Denver (DU) is working with YBP Library Services and EBL (Ebook Library) to develop a comprehensive demand-driven acquisition (DDA) plan for print and electronic monographs, with the goal of providing our students and faculty the largest pool of potential titles the university can afford. The wider range of resources will give users more choice and should make it more likely that the exact book for a particular project is available in the correct format at the point of need.

## Why Demand-Driven Acquisition Makes Sense

Collection development in academic libraries always balances competing needs, demands, and resources. With limited money, librarians attempt to purchase the correct mix of books for their students and faculty, books that will serve curricular and research needs for current and future patrons. These decisions are based on careful consideration of program size, degree level, current faculty research projects, importance of the monograph to the discipline, and existing collection strengths, among others. Against these we weigh budget constraints and shelf and storage limits, which almost always prevent a library from acquiring everything needed or wanted by its users.

Like many academic libraries in North America, the University of Denver's Penrose Library employs an approval vendor (YBP Library Services) to help manage the acquisition of English-language books. The library maintains a profile with YBP that dictates which books the library will purchase. The approval profile uses sophisticated rules based on subject, price, publisher, audience, edition, and other factors to generate weekly sets of titles likely to interest the library. Based on these rules, some books arrive automatically, others are added to notification lists, and others are blocked entirely. The library operates additional approval plans with other vendors for other languages. The approval plan is a valuable service that greatly simplifies acquisitions and saves the library a great deal of time. But the point of an approval plan – to narrow the universe of titles to a manageable number – ensures that library users will not be able to easily access most books published.

Vast numbers of books are published every year, and no library can hope to buy them all. A good estimate of the annual North American scholarly publishing output is the number of books treated on approval by an academic library book vendor. From July 1, 2009 to June 30, 2010, YBP profiled 63,145 North American titles and another 18,022 titles from the United Kingdom, or a total of 81,167. And this is less than half of total monographic publishing. The *Library and Book Trade Almanac* reports that in 2009, 175,443 titles of all sorts were published just in the United States (Barr and Harbison 2010). And UNESCO estimates that around 1,000,000 books are published worldwide annually.[1] In a typical year, the University of Denver purchases about 25,000 books from all sources and in all languages.

---

1   UNESCO Institute for Statistics, "Book Production: Number of Titles by UDC Classes, Table IV.5" Africa: http://www.uis.unesco.org/TEMPLATE/ html/CultAndCom/Table _IV_5_Africa.html; Americas: http://www.uis. unesco.org/TEMPLATE/html/CultAndCom/Table_IV_5_America.html; Asia: http://www.uis.unesco.org/TEMPLATE/html/CultAndCom/Table_IV_ 5_Asia.html; Europe: http://www.uis.unesco.org/TEMP LATE/ html/CultAnd Com/Table_IV_5_Europe.html; Oceania: http://www.uis.unesco.org/TEM

The books we buy clearly do not meet all user needs. In the 2009-2010 fiscal year, DU students, faculty, and staff requested 14,675 books through Prospector, the statewide shared catalogue, and 1,280 through interlibrary loan from other sources. Though these figures certainly include titles requested more than once as well as titles already held by DU but checked out to another user, it is clear that our users need many books not originally purchased by the library.

Conversely, many of the books in the collection are not meeting user needs. Of the 126,953 books catalogued in the five-years from 2000 through 2004, 50,226 (39.6 percent) have never circulated, even after having had at least five years to be discovered. Most books that are used at all see limited use: only 18.8 percent of the total titles have circulated four or more times (Table 1). Numerous studies have shown that this generally low rate of circulation is typical for academic libraries (see for example, Kent et al. 1979, Tyler et al. 2010, Jobe and Levine-Clark 2008, Levine-Clark and Jobe 2007).

| Number of Circulations | Titles | Percentage |
|:---:|:---:|:---:|
| 0 | 50,226 | 39.6% |
| 1 | 26,155 | 20.6% |
| 2 | 16,257 | 12.8% |
| 3 | 10,461 | 8.2% |
| 4+ | 23,854 | 18.8% |
| Total | 126,953 | |

Table 1. Collection use at the University of Denver for titles catalogued from 2001 through 2004.

As collections age, the likelihood that books will be used decreases. For the 23,527 items (on 21,356 bibliographic records) catalogued in 2000, 37.1 percent have never circulated. Since January 1, 2005, however, 54.7 percent of these books have not been used. *If books are likely to be used only in the first several years after their purchase, and ultimately are not used very much at all, it makes sense not to buy them but to lease them as needed.*

An acquisitions model in which books are purchased at the point of need based on user demand can solve some of the problems inherent in

PLATE/html/CultAndCom/Table_IV_5_Oceania.html (all accessed 1 February 2011).

prospective collection development. Instead of spending time building collections in which 40 percent or more of the books will not be used, most books that are used will be used infrequently, and older materials will see decreasing use, librarians can concentrate their energy on building larger collections of titles that can be leased or purchased at the point of need. This approach gives users a much larger pool of titles from which to choose and obviates the need to purchase books that will never be used or will be used only a handful of times.

Libraries have traditionally been forced to purchase books near the time of publication because of a combination of factors relating to discovery and publishing. Scholarly books typically go out of print fairly quickly. With tiny initial print runs and limited audiences, most academic monographs have not sold well enough to warrant a second printing. Printing too many copies of a book that delivers slender margins in the first place can be economically ruinous for the publisher. Housing and remaindering unsold copies have their own costs. As a result, publishers are quick to declare scholarly titles out of print. Because it was difficult to find out-of-print books, libraries that did not buy books right away risked losing forever the opportunity to acquire those titles.

Several factors have combined to decrease that risk significantly. The online used-book marketplace has made it easy to discover out-of-print books (Holley and Ankem 2005, Levine-Clark 2004, Tafuir 2009). More significantly, print-on-demand solutions such as Lightning Source and Custom Point mean that publishers can print single copies after the initial print run is sold out, and can even reconsider the need for a print run in the first place.[2] And as publishers move to ebooks, there will be no reason for a book ever to go out of print.

Libraries have also traditionally purchased books up-front because users based their behavior on the assumption that materials would be on the shelf. Browsing the shelves was an important way of finding books, because the finding tool – whether a card catalogue or an online catalogue – provided scant information about the book. But libraries have been dismantling that option and improving the means of discovering book content in other ways for years. As libraries have moved large

---

2   For information on Lightning Source, see http://www.lightningsource. com (accessed 4 February 2011). For information on R.R. Donnelly's Custom Point, see http://www. rrdonnelley.com/custompoint/ (accessed 4 February 2011).

portions of their collections to storage or branch libraries, have increasingly made purchasing decisions based on those of consortial partners, and have begun purchasing ebooks, it has become impossible to expect that physically browsing the shelves will provide meaningful results. It also seems likely that the best books always have been those already checked out. More importantly, the availability of ebooks and the ability to search more of the book online deliver better options for discovery. In sum, books do not need to be on the shelf.

## Demand-Driven Acquisition at the University of Denver

The University of Denver's Penrose Library has experimented with demand-driven acquisition at various times over the past decade. Like most libraries, Penrose purchases many books that are requested by faculty and students. Though a form of user-driven acquisition, this is not demand-driven acquisition. One difference is that these books are often titles that a library patron thinks should be in the collection rather than books that a user needs at the moment.

From 1999 through the end of 2005, we participated in a shared project to allow demand-driven acquisition of ebooks through NetLibrary. Members of the Colorado Alliance of Research Libraries purchased and shared access to ebooks after they had been used twice by any combination of users in the group. The Alliance acquired about 17,000 books for its users through this early experiment with demand-driven acquisition, but the project ultimately failed because the trigger for purchase (two uses of any length) did not allow for any meaningful discovery within the text, leading to purchase of many books that would likely have been rejected by a user browsing the shelf. Further, the pool of titles was not prescreened carefully by librarians, which led to the purchase of many questionable ebooks.

Over the past several years, Penrose Library has had a policy of purchasing automatically many books requested through interlibrary loan. When first implemented, this policy was simply a way to save on borrowing costs; we automatically purchased all books that cost less to buy than to borrow. Often these books were not added to the collection. We have expanded this policy to include books that may cost more to purchase than to borrow, with the intention of adding the material to the collection. The library automatically purchases all books based on a user request to ILL that meets certain criteria (publisher, price, publication date, etc.). Since a user has gone through the trouble of filling out an ILL request form, we assume that such books will be used. Several studies have shown that books purchased as the result of ILL requests circulate at a higher rate than books acquired through traditional channels (Nixon and Saunders 2010, Tyler 2010, Way 2009). And since these purchases must meet other criteria, the books should be suitable for permanent addition to the collection.

Since May 2010, Penrose Library has provided access to over 50,000 ebooks from EBL. At the point when this program started, none of these ebooks was owned by DU, and all were available for potential purchase. The library loaded records for the ebooks into the online catalogue, allowing users to discover them and trigger a short-term loan or purchase. The EBL model allows libraries flexibility in setting up a demand-driven acquisitions plan. For example, the program enables us to combine short-term loans and purchases of ebooks. At DU, the plan is configured so that ebooks are leased for 24 hours for each of the first three uses. On the fourth use, the library buys the ebook. Since most print books are used three or fewer times, it seems likely that the pattern will continue with ebooks. It is worthwhile to note, however, that since ebook and print book use are measured very differently, a direct comparison is not possible.

## Demand-Driven Acquisition of Print and Electronic Books

The University of Denver has been working closely with YBP and EBL to develop a demand-driven acquisition plan that will incorporate print and electronic books. When finalized, this plan will provide ebooks on demand from EBL and print books from YBP. Instead of ordering the books that are identified by the slip notifications from our approval plan, Penrose Library will load the records for those titles into the catalogue, allowing our users to select them as needed. The automatic approval portion of the approval plan will continue to deliver books automatically, with no patron intervention.

Demand-driven acquisition seems to be the obvious method for delivery of ebook content; ebooks can be accessed instantly upon lease or purchase, and the act of acquisition is invisible to the user. With the EBL model, the first five minutes of use are free. This discovery period – equivalent to pulling a book off the shelf to decide whether to check it out – is an important aspect of the model, preventing unnecessary purchase of unneeded material. As mentioned above, the first three uses beyond the free five-minute window allowed each person who looks at any book lead to a short-term loan, a one-day lease of the book for a small portion of the list price of the title. On the fourth use, the library purchases the ebook for the hardcover list price. If the user chooses to download the ebook at any point before the fourth use, the library automatically purchases that title. None of these various transactions is evident to the user.

Most academic books are not available yet in e-format, and many users want print books for some portion of their work. To provide a wider range of titles and to satisfy users who want a printed volume, we will expand the demand-driven acquisition plan to include the printed books for which YBP currently sends notifications. The library will load records for these books into the catalogue, allowing users to discover the titles and request purchase. The books for which YBP sends notifications already meet basic criteria that the library has indicated match collecting needs. Instead of using selectors to narrow this pool of 20,000-25,000 titles annually down to the number purchased each year (7,500-10,000 titles), users will select the titles that they need. Into the near future we will continue to receive the 7,500-10,000 books sent automatically each year.

A crucial aspect of this plan is the idea that users should be able to duplicate print and electronic books as needed. The library conducted surveys of the university community in 2005 and 2010 about ebook use.[3] One clear conclusion of the 2010 survey is that users prefer ebooks for some functions and print books for others; because people may read the same book for different purposes, different users may want the same title in different formats. A demand-driven acquisition model allows the library, whenever possible, to provide access to both formats of the same title, but only to purchase either format when

---

3   For results of the 2005 survey, see Michael Levine-Clark, "Electronic Book Usage: A Survey at the University of Denver," *portal: Libraries and the Academy* 6, no. 3 (2006): 285-299 and Michael Levine-Clark, "Electronic Book Usage and Humanities: A Survey at the University of Denver," *Collection Building* 26, no. 1 (2007): 7-14. For brief results of the 2010 survey, see Michael Levine-Clark, "Making Smart Choices: Data-Driven Decision Making in Academic Libraries," IDS Project Conference, Oswego, N.Y., August 3, 2010, http://idsproject.org/conferences/2010/Post Conference/IDS%20Data. pptx (accessed 4 February 2011).

needed. The model encourages duplication, but only duplication based on actual need.

To make the model work, YBP, EBL, and DU are developing a landing page so that a user accessing one format and attempting to trigger a purchase is informed that the other is available for purchase or use. This system should allow a user who needs information immediately, who needs to use only a small part of the book, or who wants to search within the text to use the ebook. At the same time, someone who desires to read immersively can request the print edition. In some cases the same user may wish to use the same book in both formats.

When a user accesses an ebook beyond five minutes and for purchases, checks a book out for a fourth time, the library is automatically billed for a short-term loan or a purchase. Because of the nature of the ebook format, this process is seamless. With printed books, the process is much more complicated. After the user discovers the book in the catalogue, he or she will be told that the library does not own this book, possibly that an ebook version is also available, and that it will take some time to receive a printed volume. After the book has been requested, Acquisitions staff will place a rush order, or in certain circumstances, request the book through Prospector, the statewide shared catalogue. Ultimately, this process should involve no staff mediation. Once the book is received, the library will notify the user and hold the book. Penrose Library will catalogue and process the book before checking it out to the user, but in libraries with a significant cataloguing backlog it would make sense to process the book after it is returned. Though we have discussed the notion of receiving the books pre-processed, we rejected that idea since it would add time before shipping.

Ideally, the demand-driven acquisition service would be used for most scholarly monographs, greatly expanding the pool of titles available for potential use without tying up the library budget until the point of need. However, a number of factors make it impossible to move to a demand-driven acquisitions model for all books in all formats. Most importantly, only about 17 percent of frontlist titles from academic publishers are available as ebooks within two months of their print publication, and only about 35 percent are available after a year.[4] Though the number of ebooks available is increasing, for the short term libraries will have to buy a significant number of academic books in a print

---

4    Email from Kim S. Anderson, Senior Collection Development Manager and Bibliographer, YBP Library Services, 10 March 2011.

format. Nor is it clear that users will embrace demand-driven acquisition of print books. Because print books must be shipped to the library, even a rush order will take several days to a week to arrive. An undergraduate with a paper due tomorrow will clearly reject this option, but it may prove acceptable for students and faculty with longer-term research projects.

Combining ebooks with local print-on-demand would answer the concern about shipping times by providing a fast and affordable option to print books quickly and at the point of need. However, existing print-on-demand solutions – such as the Espresso Book Machine from On Demand Books – do not yet have sufficient frontlist content to make them a viable solution.

## Assessment

To determine the effectiveness of the program, we plan to assess several aspects, including the quality and breadth of the material purchased; the best cost model for the e-book portion; and user satisfaction with the process and the content.

Because a large percentage of the titles available through the demand-driven acquisition program will be identified by means of slip notifications, one way of analyzing the books purchased on demand is to compare them with what selectors would have purchased had they ordered titles directly from the slips. Selectors will keep track of what they would have ordered during the first year of the project and will then compare what was purchased through user selection with what they would have purchased themselves. This will allow us to determine whether purchasing patterns have changed dramatically and whether a balance exists across subjects.

For at least the first year, the library will keep track of the titles purchased on demand and will analyze print and electronic overlap; any differences between the titles purchased in electronic and print form; and use of user-selected titles in comparison to titles selected by librarians.[5]

---

5    Jason Price and John McDonald have demonstrated that books purchased on demand are more heavily used than those purchased for future use. Jason Price and John McDonald, "Beguiled by Bananas? A Retrospective Study of Usage and Breadth of Patron- vs. Librarian-Acquired Ebook Collections," *Charleston Conference*, November 5, 2009. http://ccdl.libraries.claremont. edu/cdm4/item_viewer.php?CISOROOT=/lea&CISOP_TR=177 (accessed 4 February 2011).

This may tell us that we need to adjust the approval plan in some way or that we need to change the mix of print and electronic titles.

Another important consideration is what use of this model costs. Over time, we will look at the cost of short-term loans relative to purchase; the number of uses after purchase relative to the cost of short-term loans; and the ways in which purchases and short-term loans vary by subject and/or publisher. All of this can help the library to adjust the plan over time. For instance, after gathering these data, we might decide that for some subjects or publishers, it would make sense to purchase the ebook on the first use, while for others it might make sense to allow only short-term loans and never purchase the ebook. For print books, use might dictate that certain categories of material come automatically because they are almost always purchased, while other categories that currently come automatically move to the demand-driven model since they tend not to be used.

Even if this approach is logical from a financial standpoint and makes sense as a way of broadening the collection, it will not work if users do not accept it. At various points in the process, we will ask users for feedback. Those who choose not to have the library purchase a print book will be asked why they made that decision; and those who choose to have the library purchase a print book will be asked how they liked the process and whether the book arrived fast enough for them. Because accessing an ebook on-demand is seamless, there will be no separate questions about the process for ebooks. Instead, the library will continue its current practice of periodically surveying users about ebook use and satisfaction.

## Looking to the Future: Implications for Libraries, Publishers, Vendors, and Scholars

Judging from the interest among librarians, demand-driven acquisition of monographs is on its way to becoming a common means for libraries to acquire some portion of their books. If so, it has profound implications for libraries, publishers, vendors, and ultimately for library users.

DDA injects a great deal of uncertainty into the entire scholarly publishing supply chain. Publishers will be unsure of how many books they will sell; vendors will need to reconsider their service model; and libraries will have to change how they budget, how they manage the pools of titles available for purchase, and how they provide services such as interlibrary borrowing and lending.

At the most basic level, a demand-driven acquisitions model forces a fundamental reconsideration of the notion of a library collection. The collection traditionally consisted of the physical materials that a library purchased. With the advent of digital collections, it was expanded to include e-journals and databases that were leased by the library, as well as some public domain and other freely available online resources. The common factors were a collection based on pre-selection and a collection that was paid for (when a payment was required) up front. A demand-driven collection, by contrast, consists of what might be rented or purchased from a pool of material that is pre-screened for suitability for institutional curricular and research needs. A collection is now everything that we can provide access to in a reasonable timely manner.

As libraries expand demand-driven acquisition programs, the potential pool of titles they might purchase grows. Libraries need to consider how long to keep titles available to users and what sorts of rules govern inclusion in the pool. If libraries are to adopt DDA on a large scale, then we should think of the pool of titles available for potential purchase in the same way that we think about the traditional collection. The beauty of an academic library is that it has collections of books acquired over the years on the chance that they may prove useful to someone someday. Unfortunately, to build this sort of collection, we have always had to make purchase decisions at the point of publication, and many books end up never leaving the shelf. DDA allows us to build strong and lasting research collections without paying for the books until the point of need. By so doing, we can build broader and deeper collections than we ever could under the traditional acquisitions model. If DDA becomes a significant means of building research library collections, then we should keep as many titles as possible available for potential purchase as long as we can afford to.

With these considerations in mind, Penrose Library made some basic assumptions up front: (1) that titles will periodically be removed from the pool; (2) that titles that have been accessed in any way will remain in the pool longer than unused books; (3) that some series or titles will remain in the pool permanently; and (4) that books in some subjects and from certain publishers will remain in the pool longer than others. The implementation of these rules may prove difficult, but we believe the possible advantages make them worth the attempt.

The first concept – that titles must be removed from the pool periodically – is mostly a concession to fiscal reality; ultimately the library has
too much financial risk if too many titles are available. It will take some
time to figure out at what point that risk occurs for us. Already many
more titles are in the catalogue than the library could afford if they were
all somehow purchased, though it is extremely unlikely that would ever
happen. We think that the pool can get very large before the threshold of
affordability passes. Thus, we are carefully monitoring expenditures. If
necessary, we are prepared to temporarily cut off access to some titles; to
disable purchases on all titles (relying instead on short-term loans only);
or to suppress records in our OPAC but allow access from within the
vendor database. We could do this at a particular point in a fiscal year if it
appears that funds might run out. Further, safeguards built into the system
prevent too much activity by one user in a time period, preventing someone from maliciously or accidentally spending out the library's budget
in a single burst. In other words, we are watching our DDA program
closely, are prepared to act if it begins to look unsustainable, and are
taking a conservative approach, building it as we observe results.

Content-based reasons exist for removing titles from the pool. The
library may want to remove older editions of books when the new
edition is available or may remove dated material, applying different
rules for different subjects. These decisions might be made title by title
or might be made using the same profiling tools that guide the approval
plan, with the plan dictating what is removed from the collection. In a
large library with a large pool of titles available for consideration, title-
by-title removal would become a difficult process.

The second concept, that titles used by someone must remain in the
pool, is based partly on the assumption that users who have already
accessed a title will be confused and frustrated if that title is removed
from the collection and partly on the assumption that if a title is used
once it could be used again. Therefore, any EBL title that has had even
one free browse or one short-term loan will remain in the pool longer
than titles that have attracted no activity. At some point lightly used
material may need to be removed, either after it has not been accessed
for a certain time or when a later edition appears, but it should not be
removed if it has been used recently.

The third concept, that some series or titles should remain in the
pool permanently, is based on the assumption that some material is core
to a discipline even if it has not been used. Just as academic libraries
have always housed vast numbers of low-use monographs so that they

might be discovered at some point in the future, a DDA pool should include titles that may be used a century in the future. Selectors can choose to designate content for permanent potential access, other books for longer-term access, and still others for short-term access. Again, this could be accomplished with title-by-title or series-by-series analysis and decision-making by selectors, or could be managed through profiling similar to that used in an approval plan.

Concept four is that the library will apply different rules for different subjects or publishers. Books in the humanities might remain longer than books in engineering, for instance. Fairly simple rules can divide the collection into broad disciplines such as humanities, social sciences, sciences, and technology; more complex rules at the subject level can exist. Depending on the complexity of the rules, the process could be easy to manage or quite difficult. Ideally, it would not be necessary to remove material based on these sorts of criteria at all (old engineering textbooks may have more value to a particular future researcher than old philosophy monographs), but given budgetary constraints, libraries would likely prefer to remove from consideration large swaths of material in subject areas less likely to see considerable use of older material.

If libraries want to manage their collections in this way, vendors will need to develop a complex array of services to help with the flow of MARC records and the addition and removal of titles. At present, a profile generates titles available to include in the pool, which means the pool grows yearly. Our plan is not as complex as the approval plans today because we can think more broadly about what goes into the collection since the books do not have to be purchased; the point of an approval plan is to narrow the universe of titles down to what is affordable. The point of a DDA profile is to make much more of the approval universe available, knowing that many of the books will not be used and others will result only in free browses or short-term loans. In conjunction with the management of the pool of titles available for potential purchase, the vendor supplies MARC records to help with discovery. These records should be as robust as possible, including multiple points of access, such as tables of contents and links to book reviews. But the more complex piece of the vendor service is the management of what remains in the pool and what gets removed. If this is managed like an approval plan, the rules could become quite detailed. Libraries should be willing to pay for this set of services, especially since they might choose not to use the traditional book vendor supplying these services for the actual purchase of the book.

If libraries expand the concept of the collection to include every-thing that is being made available for potential purchase, then libraries should use whatever means make most sense for accessing those particular titles. After loading vendor-supplied records into the cata-logue, a library might choose to implement procedures that would include leasing some titles, purchasing others, and buying used copies or even borrowing from other libraries when print copies are desired. It is possible that none of these transactions would occur with the vendor that supplies the infrastructure to make demand-driven acquisition possible. Approval vendors must reconsider their entire business model in light of these possibilities.

There are profound implications for publishers as well. When a press publishes an academic monograph today, it can predict roughly how many copies of that book academic libraries will purchase. With demand-driven acquisition, it may be difficult to predict sales. Titles may take years to sell, if they sell at all, and many books may have a longer sales life. The difference between frontlist and backlist titles should blur and ultimately disappear. This could change how publishers consider what to publish and how they price and market books.

A marketplace that supports short-term loan of ebooks allows librar-ies to rethink the traditional interlibrary lending and borrowing functions. ILL was designed as a way for libraries to share physical collections, and it was a wonderful way to gain access to material that often could not be acquired except by sharing. But ILL is not efficient for sharing resources. It requires multiple steps, all of which have costs: the borrowing library must identify a holding library and request the item; the owning library must pull the item from the shelf, process it, package it, and ship it; the requesting library must unpack it, process it, notify the user that it has arrived, and eventually ship the book back to the owning library; and finally the owning library must check the book in and reshelve it. Digital material removes several steps, but the bor-rowing library still needs to identify a holding library, request the item, and ultimately "return" the item. The owning library needs to receive that request and process the loan in some way at the point of loan and the point of return. A much more efficient system, and one that could generate some revenue for publishers and vendors, would be a short-term loan program in which the borrowing library sends the user a URL for an ebook, and once the user accesses the ebook the library is billed for that loan. The library would negotiate with its vendor to determine loan periods, costs, and an access procedure. Ideally this would be negotiated with the same vendor supplying books through the demand-driven acquisition program.

These services require a reconsideration of how libraries, publishers, and vendors do business. All of us have evolved practices over decades and even centuries of managing print collections, many of which make no sense in a digital age. Reconsidering collection development from the perspective of demand forces us to rethink key assumptions we have made about how collections might be built.

## Conclusion

The University of Denver has experimented with several models for demand-driven acquisition of monographs: ebook plans with EBL and NetLibrary; purchase of ILL requests; and a print plan with YBP. All add a demand-driven option to traditional collection building. At this point, several barriers – the need for more ebook content, poorly developed models for demand-driven purchase of print books, and service and supply mechanisms centered on print – prevent us from treating demand-driven acquisition as the default way of collection building.

But we should be building our collections, to the greatest extent possible, through a demand-driven model. Demand-driven acquisition allows us to build broader collections that provide our users with the most material possible, making it more likely that they will find the right book for their need. At the University of Denver, we hope to embrace this model as the primary means of collection development for monographs.

For demand-driven acquisition to work on a large scale, vendors must help libraries manage the titles available to patrons. Doing so involves identifying books available for lease or purchase; providing metadata for access to these titles; and managing long-term access and removal of unused books from the pool. The model requires scalability to all sorts of libraries. The University of Denver has been working closely with YBP and EBL on our implementation of this service model, an approach that we hope will enable us to implement demand-driven acquisition as our default means of acquiring monographs.

# References

Barr, Catherine and Constance Harbison. "Book Title Output and Average Prices: 2006-2009," in Dave Bogart, ed., *Library and Book Trade Almanac 2010*. Medford, N.J.: Information Today: 485.

Holley, Robert P. and Kalyani Ankem. "The Effect of the Internet on the Out-of-Print Book Market: Implications for Libraries." *Library Collections, Acquisitions, and Technical Services* 29, no. 2 (June 2005): 118-139.

Jobe, Margaret M. and Michael Levine-Clark. "Use and Non-Use of *Choice*-Reviewed Titles in Undergraduate Libraries." *Journal of Academic Librarianship* 34, no. 4 (2008): 295-304.

Kent, Allen *et al.*, *Use of Library Materials: The University of Pittsburgh Study*. New York: Marcel Dekker, 1979.

Levine-Clark, Michael. "An Analysis of Used-Book Availability on the Internet." *Library Collections, Acquisitions, and Technical Services* 28, no. 3 (Autumn 2004): 283-297.

Levine-Clark, Michael and Margaret M. Jobe. "Do Reviews Matter? An Analysis of Usage and Holdings of *Choice*-Reviewed Titles within a Consortium." *Journal of Academic Librarianship* 33, no. 6 (2007): 639-646.

Nixon, Judith M. and Stewart E. Saunders. "A Study of Circulation Statistics of Books on Demand: A Decade of Patron-Driven Collection Development, Part 3." *Collection Management* 35, no. 3 (2010): 151-161.

Tafuri, Narda. "Libraries' Changing Buying Habits: So Many Books, So Little Money." *Against the Grain* 21, no. 5 (November 2009): 22, 24, 26.

Tyler, David C. *et al.* "Just How Right are the Customers? An Analysis of the Relative Performance of Patron-Initiated Interlibrary Loan Monograph Purchases." *Collection Management* 35, no. 3 (2010): 162-179.

Way, Doug. "The Assessment of Patron-Initiated Collection Development via Interlibrary Loan at a Comprehensive University." *Journal of Interlibrary Loan, Document Delivery & Electronic Reserve* 19, no. 4 (2009): 299-308.

# Part 2
# PDA in the World

# Chapter 4
# The Story of Patron-Driven Acquisition

Kari Paulson

*Ebook Library*

Patron-driven acquisition, or demand-drive acquisition (DDA) as we prefer to call it, really had two beginnings. In Chapter 8 Sue Polanka and Emilie Delquié describe NetLibrary's attempt. The idea was a good one, but not fully realized, and as a result did not last. Like Newton and Leibniz inventing calculus or Darwin and Wallace arriving at the idea of natural selection in different places, Ebook Library (EBL) pursued its separate path toward DDA. Where NetLibrary tried the idea in North America, EBL first explored it in Australia and Europe. All technological advances stand on the shoulders of inventions that precede them, and the shoulders upon which DDA stands are the growing acceptance of ebooks. But for the elements that have made DDA a successful alternative to established ways of buying monographs in academic libraries, the ideas of EBL's partners and the model EBL brought to market have been decisive. Put differently, I assert at the outset of this chapter, without unwarranted pride and without marketing intent that the success PDA or DDA is currently enjoying resulted largely from work that EBL did with libraries in Australia and Europe. As EBL has grown since 2004, and really since 2007, competitors have emulated or created their own variations on the approach that we and our partners pioneered, but none has discovered new elements or cobbled together a workflow that seems to work as well as the original. Thus, this chapter is about the work of only one company and its partners for the simple historical reason that these are the ideas responsible for today's DDA. What follows is the story of a collaboration whose effects are now being felt in academic and school libraries around the world.

## The Beginnings

It is unsurprising that much of the inspiration, creative thinking, and most of the ideas for the demand-driven model that EBL developed came from librarians in Australia. Australians have a deserved reputation for being pioneers and early adopters in content delivery and digital library technology. The drive for innovation is partly motivated by circumstances and partly by attitude. Australia is a western nation perched in the far corner of the eastern world, thousands of miles from western sources. And, Australia is also made up of cities that are thousands of miles from each other. Distance is a singular problem. Perhaps because of the geographical challenges, Australia's people have an in-built 'give-it-a-go' attitude that drives the innovative spirit. They are unlikely to do something just because someone insists but will try something new and, if it solves their particular problem, they will use it. If not, they will try something else. It was this 'suck-it-and-see' approach of its librarians that made Australia the perfect test bed for piloting a radically new acquisition model. It his sounds like stereotyping, but this nonetheless describes our experience of the beginnings of DDA.

Ebooks Corporation was a pioneer in ebook technology. Founded in 1997 by Australian booksellers, the company launched ebooks.com, the first dedicated e-bookstore on the web, in 2000. The company had its origins in bookselling, rather than technology, and so 'spoke the publisher language', an advantage when it came to persuading publishers to allow ebook sales of their content. Of course, many at the time were tipping ebooks as the next big thing. There were frequently cited reports by the likes of PricewaterhouseCoopers and Arthur Andersen, predicting ebook sales would comprise somewhere between 10 percent and 17 percent of the market by 2004 (or an estimated \$2.3 – 5.8 billion).[1] However, we could plainly see by our experience at ebooks.com that the predictions were wildly optimistic and that building a sustainable ebook supply chain would take time.

The company had long been thinking of building an ebook service for libraries. However, observing the slow uptake of ebooks in retail and realizing that the technology was not quite there yet (we would sell 100 ebooks in a day and receive 75 support queries), Ebooks Corporation

---

1   See, for example, Walter Crawford, "Ebook Watch," *Cites and Insights: Crawford at Large*, 1, no. 6 (June 2001): 8. Crawford himself thought the predictions were rubbish.

shelved plans until the technology began to mature. The company was also fortunate that it was not burdened by venture capital (although at the time it would not have felt that way). Founded and financed by private investors, many of whom had their background in bookselling and publishing, Ebooks Corporation could expand its products organically. We did not have hundreds of millions of dollars to work with, but if anything the lack of capital fostered inventiveness.

## Australia: Curtin University and Alison Sutherland's Persistence

It seems rare in the modern world that we can point to one person as responsible for a widely influential idea, but DDA as we know it today may not have happened had it not been for the persistence and encouragement of Alison Sutherland, a West Australian who at the time was Bibliographic Services Librarian at Curtin University. Sutherland recalls, "There was a great deal of interest in establishing the use of ebooks for the many students at Curtin University, both online and on campus, in Perth and anywhere else in the world where our students were based."[2] She first met with Ebooks Corporation in 2001, when she was invited to speak with local academics who were keen to have ebooks and who were talking to Ebooks Corporation about creating a service for libraries. Sutherland was interested to find out more about the proposal. Yet, despite interest in ebooks among the local library community, little momentum resulted from these initial meetings.

Undeterred, Sutherland's enthusiasm and commitment to the project grew. She was aware of the existing ebook platforms for libraries, but she wanted something more flexible and more responsive to their use requirements. She wanted a model that could provide multiple-concurrent access for titles they bought, and beyond this, she wanted a model where the library could have the widest selection of ebooks on demand for their students. Sutherland says, "My thinking was that we had a closed reserve collection of high-demand material that formed required reading for tutorials and coursework. This collection would be in demand for a week or two, and then would wait for the next time a chapter was called for. This was high-demand work for the library,

2    This and quotations that follow are from personal communication with Alison Sutherland, 20 May 2011.

frustrating for the students as they fought to access their books, and the material was locked up during peak times. A perfect solution would be an ebook, I thought, and then was dismayed to find that an ebook could only be read by one person at one time rather than being available for many."

Sutherland outlined her frustrations and desires and Ebooks Corporation set about trying to engineer a solution. Sutherland made clear that one of the difficulties for libraries is knowing which books best support their patrons; she understood that a line could exist between the preferences of librarians and the interests of patrons. Through their work with e-journals and large bundles that were being made available, the Curtin library had learned that some titles librarians would never have considered for purchase were being used extensively and legitimately by academics, students, and researchers, while other titles long held to be essential were not being used at all. At the same time, the library was also struggling to expend its total monograph budget.

Sutherland's insights were in many ways the key to developing DDA. First, she began to wonder about the possibility of loading ebook titles into the library OPAC, making them searchable and available to the researcher, but without purchase until certain parameters were met. Purchases would be triggered upon use, behind the scenes, automatically with no intervention or manual administration. Most important from the view of the patron, there would be no awareness or knowledge that any of this was happening. Sutherland and her colleagues at Curtin worked very closely with EBL to refine the details of the platform. They outlined workflows for MARC ingestion, request mediation, and administrative tools. Curtin wanted to be able to refine the ebook range down to specific academic publishers, and agreed that once a client had "borrowed" a title, it would be considered purchased, and the library would be invoiced. But borrowing meant much more than just a quick look.

EBL incorporated the details into its initial specifications, forming the framework of the demand-driven model in the EBL platform. It is thanks to the ideas and feedback from the Curtin library that we were able to work through the detail necessary to build a robust platform and the beginning of a DDA framework for ebooks.

## The European Perspective: CERN

CERN, which straddles Switzerland and France, is a particle physics research institution mainly employing experimental physicists, theoretical physicists, computer scientists, engineers, and administrative support staff. It is also widely known as the inventor of the World Wide Web. The institution is most recently famous for the experiments it carries out with the Large Hadron Collider and its quest to find the 'God Particle'.

Our introduction to the CERN library came through a serendipitous email from Jens Vigen, then Scientific Information Officer and now Head Librarian at CERN. The year was 2002, and Vigen had written to the support department at ebooks.com, looking for help with trouble he was having in trying to allow network access to an ebook he had purchased for one of his patrons. He wanted to load the ebook to his network to enable patrons of the CERN library to share access to the title. His query came to me from the support team, and I gently explained that, as the book was a retail sale, it was for individual use only. But I also explained that we were developing an ebook service for libraries. It seemed a long-shot that an institution responsible for the very technology our company was founded on (the Web) would be interested in collaborating with a small ebook technology firm perched on the wrong side of Australia. Nonetheless, I asked Vigen to share his ideas with us about how an ideal ebook library model and platform would look. He responded, saying that indeed he was interested in sharing his ideas.

As it turned out, CERN had been a pioneer in networking access to pre-print materials. In the 1950s they created the CERN Document Server to centralize searching of a vast array of scientific content. Additionally, Vigen and his colleagues at the CERN library had long been vocal advocates for open access and leaders in digital library technology. CERN had more complicated challenges than just distance. They had to facilitate access to content for the world's leading physicists. The library's philosophy was to provide whatever materials researchers needed as quickly as possible. Already aspiring to just-in-time access, they aimed to serve out what their scientists needed when they needed it. They were one of the early libraries to load records in their catalogue and to source requests from Amazon, BookFinder.com, and AddAll. com, using rush ordering as an alternative to inter-library loan (Vigen 2003). They had to be clever, thrifty, and nimble, able to deliver books that would probably be used only once or twice.

Vigen and his colleagues saw great possibilities for ebooks in their environment. They shared Sutherland's vision of purchasing on demand, but wanted to take the access-on-demand formula one step further and introduce an option to 'rent' the book on a pay-per-view basis before buying. They recognized the diverse nature of research and that often a book needed by one researcher bore no relation to what any other researcher needed. They wanted to build a system that identified real-time use trends and automatically purchased content where patterns of high use emerged. They hoped to build a profiled selection of content likely to be of interest to their researchers, add the records to the CERN Document Server, pay for each use, and if a pattern of demand emerged, automatically buy the titles at a designated trigger point. The idea was scientific, evidence-based acquisition. The model would enable the library to stretch its limited funds, opening access to a wider range of material with highest expenditure going toward titles with the highest use.

Besides being a way to get the latest content in front of their re-searchers, Vigen saw the model as a potential alternative to inter-library loan (ILL). We thought the idea worthy enough to write a paper and present it to the IFLA Inter-lending and Document Supply Conference in Canberra in 2003.[3] The question we posed was, why take a book off the shelf, pack it up, ship it halfway across the globe (meanwhile making it unavailable for anyone at the sending library), pack it back up to return, and risk loss or damage to the book, all at a growing cost to both libraries? Clearly, a digital lending model that cost less than buying the book and no more than packing and shipping it while delivering to the patron immediately was more promising. Could it be, we asked, that such a service as the one EBL was designing could serve as a big ILL library, providing access faster and cheaper, removing the potential for damage or loss, and reducing the environmental footprint?

We were persuaded that the case for such a model for library services was clear and that it also offered a compelling value proposition for publishers. Expenditure trends showed that rapidly growing use of ILL meant lots of money was being spent to access content, but publishers

---

3    Kari Paulson and Jens Vigen, "E-books and interlibrary loan: an academic centric model for lending," *Proceedings of the 8th IFLA Interlending and Document Supply International Conference: Breaking Barriers: Reaching Users in a Digital World*, 30 Oct. 2003, Canberra, Australia. Available at http://www.nla.gov.au/ilds/abstracts/ebooksand.htm.

were excluded from this economy. The new ebook model offered publishers a means to be included in a new incremental revenue stream.
With print ILL, the money created profits only for a courier; an ebook
lending model could redistribute revenue into the information industry
in a way that would be good for patrons, libraries, publishers, and
suppliers. The statistics uncovered as part of the research for our paper
ultimately turned out to be instrumental to the argument we presented to
publishers when encouraging them to agree to work with us.

We now had a fully formed model for DDA which included various
options for pay-per-view access and automatic purchasing based on uses.
The model could sit snugly beside traditional title-by-title purchasing.
We shared the ideas with Sutherland and our other advising libraries. It
was time to find the content needed to bring DDA to life.

## Persuading Publishers to Come Aboard

Selling the DDA model to publishers was no straightforward pitch in
the beginning. Having watched the chain of events in the music industry
as it marched into the digital realm, and having little evidence on which
to base their decisions, publishers were deeply concerned about the
potential for cannibalization and piracy. Their concerns were magnified
in the library market where they feared that one digital copy of a title
could be accessed by hundreds or thousands of users in remote locations,
replacing multiple sales with a single copy. To suggest that their titles
should be fully browsable before purchase and then made available at a
fraction of list price was neither an idea they were contemplating nor a
model in which they compellingly felt the need to participate.

We knew from the outset that our role as an aggregator was to
finely balance the hopes and desires of libraries alongside the commercial concerns of publishers. For this reason, we recruited a handful of
influential publishers as advisors, ones who were already working with
us through ebooks.com and who were well along the road in digital
distribution or the conversation about it. If we could find support among
the thought-leaders in academic publishing, it would help down the line
when approaching the hundreds of publishers we would need to have in
the catalogue.

Just as we relied on a network of libraries to shape ideas on DDA
functionality, we relied on a select network of publishers to provide
critical feedback that aligned the model with commercial realities. We

sent the publishers proposed business models and terms at various stages of development, talked with them frequently, and invited some to focus groups with librarians. We discussed and debated, and made changes and compromises along the way. Christophe Chesher at Taylor and Francis, Michael Holdsworth at Cambridge University Press, David Wynn at Oxford University Press, Kim Zwollo at Kluwer, and Elizabeth Weiss of Allen and Unwin were some of the many who were generous with their time and came to the discussions with open minds.

As the dialogue progressed, common concerns emerged, such as:

– Would the DDA model encourage libraries to spend less overall – to replace sales of full books with partial sales – further eroding monograph budgets?
– Would the browse period essentially be the same as giving content away; would patrons find what they needed during the free browsing and not need to trigger a rental of the book? An often quoted report by NetLibrary concluded that users were spending an average of less than 11 minutes in a book (Connaway and Snyder 2005). Given this statistic, was 5 minutes too generous?
– How would the publishers handle partial sales? Could their accounting and reporting systems cope with fractional sales, and did their contracts with authors allow them?

While we had no use data yet, we already had a number of good arguments in favor of at least trying the model:

– DDA provided critical mass. While the argument we were hearing from libraries at the time was that students were not using ebooks, it was clear from sales statistics that the libraries were not buying many ebooks. Here was a chicken and egg dilemma. DDA could provide a test bed to determine actual demand for ebooks by putting a critical mass of content in front of the end users. If they still did not use ebooks, we would be all the wiser.
– Title-by-title selection and transactions, as opposed to subscription, were truer to how publishers traditionally transacted with their customers. Payment had a one-to-one relation with use, and publishers were paid each time their book was used or bought. The approach was cleaner than working on a subscription algorithm.
– DDA offered an alternative to ILL. Clear and growing evidence, along with common sense, showed that as monograph budgets

decreased, expenditure on ILL increased. The trend was bad for publishers because a growing economy existed that publishers had no part in. DDA, in particular the short-term-loan access model, offered publishers an opportunity to enter this economy and to reclaim some of the funds that were going to couriers.

− DDA offered potential long-tail revenue. The DDA and short-term loan model might breathe life back into books that were considered to be out of print, out of fashion, or just out of sight where libraries were concerned. Valuable backlist content could potentially produce revenue for much longer, even indefinitely. In libraries that depend on approval plans for their buying, any book not chosen during the first round of acquisition with DDA now had a second chance of being rented or bought.

As we expanded the discussion to the wider publishing community, many said no or elected to wait and see. However, assent was widespread enough among publishers who understood why they should participate to give us good content with which to begin. Quite often, when other publishers saw the list of those already signed on, they knew that the right questions had been asked. We launched EBL in mid-2004 with about 15,000 titles. By early 2006, we had 40,000 titles in the catalogue and more coming each day from important publishers – enough to make DDA interesting.

The job of persuading publishers became easier as data accumulated. In the beginning, we had to build a proposal that relied on identifying trends in the market in general and had to ask publishers to take a leap of faith. Fortunately, the real sales and use figures clearly supported the argument. Libraries providing a critical mass of content to their users through DDA were seeing exponentially higher use of ebooks than in the past. Libraries using DDA as a primary acquisitions tool were spending far more on ebooks than those who were using traditional methods, and because of the absolute return on their investment, continued to commit larger portions of their acquisitions budgets to ebooks and books in general. The statistics helped reinforce the decision of those publishers already participating and helped us to persuade those who were awaiting data.

## Going Live

EBL officially launched at the ALA Annual Conference in 2004. Based on the ideas and on feedback from Curtin and CERN and from other advising libraries (North Carolina State University, Yale University, the Council for Australian University Libraries), we launched a system that included most of the features available through EBL and through any usable DDA workflow today. These features included:

- The ability to make books libraries did not own available to patrons.
- A substantial browse period to enable patrons to decide whether a book can help them. The browses have no cost to the library.
- Short-term loans (STLs) are our term for an approach that enables libraries to borrow a book at a small percentage of its list price. Use patterns in academic libraries show that many books on the shelf never circulate and that a high percentage circulates rarely. The STL greatly extends the number of titles available, making libraries better.
- Customizable settings and triggers, such as the ability to mediate or automate requests for non-owned titles, the choice to set an automatic-purchase after any number of STLs, and alerts to notify staff of transactions or requests.
- Multiple concurrent readers for all titles, mostly at list price, again extending library budgets.
- Books that are downloadable to computers and ebook readers.

The new service amounted to a much more flexible access model than had been available, one that we thought would greatly benefit libraries, users, and publishers alike, but we had no proof. The concept was radical and pushback from libraries was considerable. Libraries could see the benefit of paying less for the content on the periphery of their collections. They were, however, concerned about the potential of spending money on things they ultimately did not own and were deeply concerned about how their selectors would respond. Some hypothesized that users would run out of control, spending far too much and accessing wholly inappropriate content.

As EBL went live, Curtin University was beta testing the service. Sutherland says, "There were restrictions so that if the take-up had been more than we anticipated we would increase the borrow number to five or six. If the budget was blown too quickly then we would stop. But at trial all was smooth, from our point of view, for EBL, and for our patrons." Ironically, owing to internal changes at Curtin the vision did not come to fruition. Sutherland's colleagues were concerned by the demand-driven aspect and worried that students would use ebook titles that were not academically based.

Thus, to our dismay and Alison Sutherland's, Curtin decided against rolling out the demand-driven model in the way she envisioned. Rather than load MARC records into the catalogue, Curtin elected only to make content visible in the EBL platform. Rather than let patrons have immediate access to non-owned content, Curtin decided to mediate every request and decided against short-term loans, preferring only to buy content. The implementation fell far short of our shared hopes. CERN implemented the DDA workflow in January 2006, but as the library is inherently so specialized, the profile of titles they made available to their users was quite limited. To give DDA the shakedown it needed, we had to seek another partner.

## Swinburne Champions DDA

We met Gary Hardy, Associate Director, Information Support Services at Swinburne University of Technology, at the Victoria Academic Library Association (VALA) in Melbourne in early 2006. Alison Sutherland and I presented the new model at the Conference. By then, it felt to us as if the idea had been around forever, but no one had yet implemented it on a large scale. Hardy was in the audience and was instantly interested. He says of the moment, "I remember hearing you talk about the patron-driven model at a publisher forum in a room in Crown, and having a sort of recognition that what you were proposing was really the next logical step, the missing bit, that would move us forward and address some of the dysfunctions in our provision of relevant content to our users. We knew that we had to give it a try."[4]

Hardy recognized that convenience and immediacy are highly valued by many of their network-savvy patrons accustomed to identifying and instantly obtaining text material. The library's print collection struggled to meet those expectations. Again, Hardy says,

---

4    This and quotations that follow are from personal communication with Gary Hardy, 18 May 2011.

It had always been obvious to us that the model of our librarians choosing titles was a sort of hit-and-miss affair, but with the cumbersome library system we had at the time, the extent to which this was the case was largely obscured. Even with our new library system, it is still hard to get a clear idea of how successful our selection processes are. When do you start counting, from time of order? From the time an item is on the shelf? Just because someone borrows a book, do we know that they actually open the covers, or do they just carry it around, hoping some of the content will get into their brains by osmosis? Were they borrowing the book because the book they really wanted was on loan or not in the collection? We would argue in-house about use or about browsing of the shelves, with people buying for next semester saying it is not fair to count use this semester. I guess we had never developed a methodology for clearly identifying the effectiveness of our selection, nor the reports to give us a real picture of how we were tracking.

"Ironically," continues Hardy, "it was reports from the use of content acquired under another ebook model that drove home to us the limitations of our selection processes. Under this other model, we could select a fixed number of titles from a list of available ebooks. Using our best selection efforts, the reports showed us that more than 30% of the titles we chose were never used." The number was unacceptable.

Hardy and his colleague Tony Davies tracked down Sutherland to discuss her original vision. They concluded that putting too much effort into trying to pick content beforehand basically broke the model. Users either knew what they wanted, or they did not; either they wanted the sort of content librarians thought it was the library's business to provide, or they did not. In the library's internal discussions a divide was discernable, with optimists who thought patrons were a sensible bunch who would buy sensible things, and pessimists who prophesied that use-driven acquisition would waste money buying a load of "odd, off-topic bilge." As Hardy explained,

We were concerned that one or a few obsessive users could monopolize the purchasing. We were worried about the users running suddenly amok and spending a big chunk of our budget before we could react. Essentially, we were worried about making a mistake. One very strong strand in the librarian psyche is a deep desire not to make mistakes. Our argument for the internal doubters was to point out that we make plenty of very expensive collection-development mistakes already – we need to balance the relatively low cost of a poor patron-driven ebook choice (which at least one of our users wanted) against the much steeper cost of selecting, acquiring, processing, cataloguing, housing, and then disposing or putting into indefinite storage a physical item that nobody might ever want.

In July 2006 Swinburne became the first library to load the entire EBL list (just more than 34,000 thousand records at the time) into their catalogue and allow unmediated short-term loans and automatic un-mediated purchasing of ebooks.[5] Swinburne made no distinction where patrons were concerned between items that the library had yet to acquire and books the library owned. Patrons could browse, read online, and download any EBL ebook. Patrons borrowed non-owned titles as short-term loans and the library paid a percentage of the list price for these. Swinburne set an automatic purchase trigger to buy any title the third time someone wanted to borrow it.

Hardy points out that one factor helping Swinburne to adopt the DDA model was their relatively modest collection budget. There was no argument that they did not own most of the content EBL could provide; the pool of EBL titles represented a significant expansion to the scope of Swinburne's collection, which made it very attractive if it proved affordable. Swinburne also had the advantage of being relatively small, which made getting some things done easier than in a larger management structure. They were able to work up a pilot without having to persuade any committee or wider group. Their approach was to allocate a budget; work out an exit strategy that they could imple-ment if things went 'pear shaped'; set the level at which mediation would be required conservatively; and watch what was happening very, very closely.

Swinburne entered boldly but not blindly. They identified initial questions, issues, and decisions. Coming to the decision to proceed required overcoming many anxieties:

- How much would this cost?
- With only basic MARC records would patrons be able to find the ebooks in the catalogue?
- Would patrons select the right sort of material?
- Some patrons do not like ebooks; would offering them ebooks be a problem?
- What about duplicates?
- How would they handle DDA updates and deletions?

---

5   Brown University of Rhode Island in the United States experimented with DDA at about the same time as Swinburne but did not continue after their pilot study.

- What would they do if the DDA workflow was not sustainable?
- How could they get the optimal return within the budget?

At the beginning Swinburne really had no idea what DDA would cost. From July to December, their designated pilot phase, they spent close to $55,000 US, somewhat more than they anticipated. Hardy recalls, "There were anxious conversations during some of the busier weeks, where the rate of expenditure seemed to rise alarmingly." Yet, Hardy and his colleagues could see almost immediately that the patrons were looking at ebooks entirely appropriate to Swinburne's teaching and research profile.

Analysis of results revealed interesting trends and provided further support for the model. For example, overall use of EBL titles proved to be an example of the long tail (a characteristic that has been borne out over and over) – a relatively small number of titles are used extensively, but a large range of titles will be used some if left in the catalogue over a long period, and taken together, their use is significant. The ability to offer these titles, thanks to short-term loans, made the library better. The library spent $31,502 on 4,195 short-term loans (representing 3,075 titles and 59% of total pilot expenditure) and $22,100 buying 296 titles (41% of total pilot expenditure).

Besides the short-term loan charges and automatic-purchase charges the library firm ordered 24 titles during July and August 2006, totaling $1,540 US. The use of these manually purchased titles provided an interesting comparison to those automatically purchased on the third DDA use. Thirteen of the 24 titles that were firm ordered had zero use by the end of the year, and only three of the titles would have triggered an automatic purchase. The library also found that their ebooks purchased on demand had a much higher circulation rate than the print books they purchased in the same period, with far fewer print books circulating at all after purchase.

Early responses from Swinburne's users were intriguing. Hardy says that,

As we were loading so many ebook records into the catalogue, inevitably some of our users noticed that the ratio of ebooks to physical books had changed, and we received some negative feedback, people saying, 'I don't want the library to be acquiring ebooks; I want physical books'. Our response then, as now, is that essentially the choice is not between an ebook and a physical book, but rather between an ebook and no book. We simply could not afford to provide access to the same range of titles that we do if we did not deploy the DDA model.

## Swinburne has used DDA ever since that first trial. Says Hardy,

> Subsequent experience has confirmed our intuitive sense that DDA is a very effective way of building our collection. It has not been without challenges. Implementing a new discovery tool plus adding more titles to the selection pool led to a sharp spike in our spending on DDA titles. Having the range of titles available has changed purchasing by our collection-development librarians; why buy from your budget if the users can decide if they want a particular title? DDA has helped deconstruct our traditional resources budget. Where, salami-like, we sliced our resources budget into individual departments and disciplines according to an arcane formula and pursued the selectors to spend their budgets, we now have one bucket and an instruction to 'buy what you need'.

Although use during the pilot turned out to be slightly higher than the library initially expected, they concluded that the model was affordable, and they had a basis for their 2007 budget. Hardy and his colleagues at Swinburne decided to move out of the pilot phase and implement demand-driven acquisition as their primary acquisition model. The library was seeing things in a new way, asking themselves, for example, whether they should look at titles that were automatically purchased in EBL as a tool to identify where they should buy print titles.

Hardy and Davies were quick to share their pilot results with the Australian library community. They published a paper and presented it to a packed auditorium at the Australian Library and Information Association (ALIA) Conference in Sydney in January 2007.[6] Word of the project spread fast, and soon many Australian libraries were ready to set-up pilots of their own. This good idea, our collective hunch, was becoming a legitimate model, backed up by real statistics and experience. Hardy puts it colorfully when he says, "I think Swinburne taking the plunge, being the first penguin off the iceberg and not getting eaten by a killer whale, encouraged others in our community to dive in as well."

---

6   Gary Hardy and Tony Davies, "Letting the patrons choose: using EBL as a method for unmediated acquisition of ebook materials," *[Proceedings] Information Online 2007: 13th Australian Library and Information Association (ALIA) Exhibition and Conference, Sydney, New South Wales, Australia, 30 January-01 February 2007*. Available at http://researchbank.swinburne.edu.au/vital/access/services/Download/swin:5065/DS2.

## Influence and Adoption

Today in Australia and New Zealand, DDA is a relatively common practice and still gaining ground. We work with the majority of academic libraries in Australia and New Zealand and nearly 62% of the academic libraries are using some form of DDA with EBL, many, like Swinburne, for four or more years now. We are only recently seeing this kind of adoption and dialogue taking shape in the United States and growing interest and adoption in the United Kingdom. In Europe, with some exceptions in, for example, the Netherlands and Scandinavia, DDA has been slower to catch on but interest is growing.

So far, we have been impressed and often surprised by the different creative approaches to designing profiles, modifying settings, or managing expenditure. Each library adds its own signature to the program, using different metrics or criteria for adding or culling content or increasing or decreasing expenditures. And just as the libraries have been generous with us in sharing ideas about what works and what does not, they have been generous in sharing ideas and information with each other.

DDA is a natural for any library that lacks space, that must build an opening-day collection, or that needs to use its resources efficiently. Ebooks are less costly to acquire than print, and ebooks are no longer exotic. The idea of use-driven acquisition, where libraries can show more books than they could afford to buy, is powerful. More publishers are seeing the advantage of having books on the virtual shelves of dozens of libraries rather than on the shelves of the few that can afford to buy them outright. In effect, DDA is an idea whose time has come thanks, above all, to the vision of a few people in Australia and Europe.

## References

Connaway, Lynn Silipigni, and Clifton Snyder. "Transaction Log Analyses of Electronic Book (eBook) Usage." *Against the Grain. 17* (February 2005): 85-89.

Vigen, Jens. "What Attracts Clients to Your ILL Service in a Global Market?" *Fifth Nordic Interlending Conference: ILL in a Digital Age – Challenges, Barriers, Opportunities.* http://cdsweb.cern.ch/record/585088/files/open-2002-058.html (Accessed 6 June 2011).

# Chapter 5
# Building New Libraries on the International Stage: The Near and Middle East

Rex Steiner
*Azerbaijan Diplomatic Academy, Baku, Azerbaijan*
and
Ron Berry
*New York University, Abu Dhabi*

In the developed world, number of volumes has long been a measuring stick for libraries, so it is unsurprising that the developing world has usually adopted that view. In new international libraries, collection development strategies have historically been focused on print collections. The history of these libraries has been one of equating huge print collections with a vast possession of knowledge by the owner of the library. You could see, smell, and touch the knowledge in a library of print books. When building a new university, among the first things the benefactor wants is a huge library filled with impressive volumes of print books that show off the young university's knowledge in the form of paper and steel. The challenge for new institutions is to let go of this traditional ideal. We believe that adopting the PDA model is a great help in building a new library quickly and with vast financial and time savings. But perhaps more important, it helps to shift the ideas of the benefactors away from print and steel, to something that is, oddly perhaps, more durable. PDA allows skeptics to experiment with ebooks at very little risk – many of the skeptics we have dealt with have rarely used an ebook and view them primarily as glorified PDF documents. But once they see what can be done with ebooks, that they are not simply long PDF's, many users – sometimes begrudgingly – accept that ebooks have a significant place in the collection.

## Background

In this chapter we will describe experiences at two libraries in the Middle East and one in the Caucasus.[1] For each we will present a summary of the practices during the times when the library was preparing for its opening day. As the times changed, so did the outlook, but often, the factor that dictated the development of the collection was technology.

As the story of these libraries begins the best technology around that would support a curriculum was paper books. Librarians could see the potential of ebooks, but in the late 1990s, enough content simply was not available. No matter how hopeful we were about the arrival of ebooks, it was apparent that it was not the time of the ebook. The next stage of new library development, beginning about 2005, had a much more focused notion of ebooks, thanks in part to the availability of other electronic resources. The ebook really had not begun to reach its full potential, but it was obviously coming, thanks in part to better content and better Internet technology. But, it was still too early to put a great deal of focus on the electronic. Print remained king.

Today, however, it is obvious that the time has come to seriously look at the ebook option and the benefits it can bring. Developing a new library today can mean taking a blank canvas and creating something new and better; unlike in the past, old print-focused models do not have to predominate. Today, the library-as-warehouse does not hold sway. Advances in technology, content, and acquisition models mean that there can be an effective blend of electronic and print, with the future leaning toward the electronic. As romantic (and valid) as it once was to be able to walk into a library and enjoy the aesthetic value of a grand print collection, it appears the libraries of the future will be of a very different character (perhaps better, perhaps worse – but surely different). Over the past ten years, the landscape has changed in the international library world, and in this overview we touch on the experience of developing libraries in emerging cultures.

---

1   Editor's note. The authors of this chapter have spent most of the past ten years working in start-up libraries in far-flung parts of the world. They worked together at the American University of Sharjah (AUS), then each worked at different libraries. To make clear the "I" of each section we have named the writer. In the final section they draw together their united con-clusions based on the time at AUS and through their different posts.

# The American University of Sharjah
*Rex Steiner and Ron Berry*

Today, the American University of Sharjah (AUS) is the jewel in the crown of University City in the tiny Emirate of Sharjah that adjoins Dubai in the United Arab Emirates. AUS has a grand library, capped by a beautiful dome, that is in many respects the standard for libraries in the region and whose history illustrates the possibilities that have dawned in the past decade.

In 1997, His Highness Dr. Sheikh Sultan bin Mohammad Al Qasimi of Sharjah had the vision of using the wealth of his Emirate to build a world-class education system so that his people did not have to leave the country to attend university. Many traditional families in this family-first culture did not like sending their children to far-off places such as North America or Europe. They wanted their children to have a western-style education, but not be exposed to the elements of western society of which they disapproved. As a result, Dr. Sheikh Sultan decided to create a campus where his people, and eventually people of other Arabian Gulf nationalities, could obtain a western-style education without leaving home.

A key part of the AUS campus, and a signature piece of the university, was to be the library. After officials selected a location on the outskirts of Sharjah where the campus (and later, University City) would have room to grow, the building began. In the original plans, the largest, most significant building, the library, was a huge domed structure – visible from anywhere on campus and having a grand and imposing overview of the entire University City. The infrastructure of the building was to be 100 percent electronic and was to contain no paper volumes whatsoever. It was a forward-thinking approach for 1997, and indeed, beyond practicality at the time. As the building was developed and staff were hired, it became apparent that a paper-free library was not a realistic option – not enough electronic material, especially books, existed to support the curriculum.

With an all-electronic library impractical, the building had to be reconfigured to create space for shelving and for the acquisition of printed books, a major redesign. As it became clear that the library was going to be a more traditional print collection, the original four-floor plan became a one-floor library at the top of the building. The loss of floor space meant recalculating acquisitions targets. At the time, a goal of libraries in the area was to have "one-million-volumes" as quickly as possible, but at one floor, this was not going to be one of those libraries.

With the evolution of the plan from no print books to tens of thousands of books, other factors came into play. The structure itself was not designed for the weight of a print-based library. The extreme weight of the steel and paper on the fourth floor began to cause concerns about the overall stress to the structure itself. Load-bearing formulas had to be recalculated, and major additions to the entire structure were required. Once the structural challenges were overcome, it was time to focus on collection-building.

The library acquired books as quickly as possible. When moved from its temporary facility to the new donut-shaped floorplan, about 9,000 volumes were in the collection, a modest number that took up a fraction of the space available in the library. As the shelves were acquired and assembled, it became apparent that books needed to be amassed much more quickly. Acquiring 9,000 volumes had taken more than two years, far too slow to reach the long-term acquisitions target of 100,000 in less than 10 years. Acquisitions had to be doubled and doing so required assembling a team of experienced librarians and a vendor that could deliver shelf-ready volumes.

As the library team was assembled and the revised collection-development plan took shape, it became obvious that certain things had to be accounted for that were not originally required. The cost of building the library had already exceeded the projections in the original plan. In addition to the increased cost for acquiring more books themselves, the library was faced with new costs such as shelving, processing fees for shelf ready volumes, and substantial shipping costs of roughly 10 percent on top of the total acquisitions budget. Additional staff members were added specifically to select and then receive the new volume of materials. With the new realities, the library needed almost 10 years and millions of dollars to reach their acquisitions targets. (Had an option like PDA been available, the acquisitions target could have been reached practically overnight with minimal investment.) Fortunately, the University's benefactor was a major supporter of the library and most of these initial cost obstacles were overcome without great difficulty. However, one thing that was overlooked when the library's focus changed from electronic to print was preservation. Because this was a first-of-its kind endeavor in the small Gulf kingdom, the oversight was understandable.

## Saving the Books

As the library soon discovered, the print books needed special care and attention. In the original design of the library building at AUS, the heating, ventilation, and air-conditioning (HVAC) systems were set up according to a specification that is common in office buildings in the region. What was not considered was humidity control. No one could have expected the effects this oversight would have on the collection. Intense summer temperatures and high humidity soon gave rise to mildew, with ruinous effects. Shortly after the library space was fully opened, staff began to notice white and green mold on the chairs and some of the cloth-bound books. It became clear that not only had extra precautions not been taken to reduce humidity, but that areas of the library that did not house books were not air conditioned at all, which dramatically increased overall humidity, making an ideal breeding ground for mold. As this was discovered, the library had a growing collection that already represented a significant financial investment by the university (worth at least $2 million USD). To protect the books, the library staff moved quickly to eradicate the mold and modify the HVAC systems, at significant expense.

## The New Library

AUS quickly became a success. As Dr. Sheikh Sultan hoped, local families sent their sons and daughters to the university, but AUS also became a favored destination for students from the entire region and even farther afield. One result of this growth was that after only a couple of years it became apparent that a new single-purpose building was needed for the library. In 2002, preliminary research was done to construct a library intended to fulfill the needs of all the University community. Things came full-circle and much like in the original plan, the library was to be a grand structure and occupy a central and commanding location on the campus. Two central needs were identified in the planning process:

1.  The need for an active and flexible learning space for students and faculty. The learning spaces were and continue to this day to be a great success, as evidenced by the traffic and user satisfaction with the library.

2. Room for the print collection, including a modest plan for accommodating growth with the necessary square feet of shelving. Planning for the growth of the collection followed many of the standard metrics at the time, print titles added per year and linear feet of shelving to suitably accommodate the collection over the years.

As these plans were made, the ebook industry still had not reached a point that would serve the needs of the library. The bundled packaging of a broad range of titles or selected publishers was the norm with the possibility of individual purchase of selected titles. The advent of a viable and sustainable platform for PDA was in its infancy and its effects on a variety of library services was unrecognized.

It is interesting to speculate what would have happened had an ebook PDA plan been available in the early days. Money would have been saved, of course. But even more interesting is that the collection, in essence, would have begun to build itself electronically rather physically. Different decisions may have been made regarding allocations of space for a physical collection. More space could have gone to students.

## The Petroleum Institute
*Rex Steiner*

Beginning in 2006, I was involved in the creation and development of another new library, this time in the Emirate of Abu Dhabi. This was a special library devoted to science and technical topics covering electrical, chemical, mechanical, and petroleum engineering, along with the geosciences. At the time of my arrival, the library had about 8,000 books donated from a previously closed institution. The books had no order, and they were housed on locally made shelves that could not be moved or adjusted. Our immediate focus was two-fold:

1. Select an ILS and implement it so that we could use the small collection that we already had, an issue we were able to address quickly, with the full support of the administration.
2. Select a book vendor that could provide shelf-ready material in the numbers that we needed

Ebooks were still in their infancy. We were interested in obtaining them but doing so was organizationally difficult. First, we faced a strict adherence to buying locally if possible, impractical when your needs are books and specialized services such as cataloguing, label printing, MARC, and so forth for each. No local vendor could do this, but before using an international book vendor, we had to follow the rules of procurement. The rules included a three-bid requirement, which meant that each book needed to have three vendors bid, and the lowest price won the right to sell the book. The usual process was to fax (only fax bids were allowed) the list of books to at least three local book suppliers. The suppliers looked over the lists, and prices for each book, and then returned the list by the deadline. The library staff would then look over the bids and select the low-priced bidder for each book.

For the library staff the procedure meant enormous work creating, reviewing, and sending lists to vendors; waiting for responses; reviewing returned lists; selecting the lowest bidder for each book; sending out the order to the winning bidder; and then waiting for up to four weeks to acquire each title. Once we obtained the book we had to catalogue and process it ourselves. The entire process could easily take three months to put even one book on the shelf. Indeed, books ordered routinely went out of print before we obtained them.

The three-bid system was a budget nightmare as well. Money would be encumbered for months, and then books would be unavailable, which meant getting the funds back in the budget. By the end of our first fiscal year it was apparent that it was practically impossible to a) acquire the number of books we needed; and b) to expend the budget. Because we were having difficulty growing the collection and expending the budget, the administration began to ask why.

Only after two years of doing the numbers, did the library team finally persuade the administration that better ways of acquiring books existed, especially through the use of a preferred vendor.

A problem we initially faced when trying to get ebooks under the "three-bid" system was that there were not three vendors available. The vendors that were available and had representatives in the region had very little science and technology material. We had no real choice but to build a print collection. When we built and planned new libraries (the institution went on to build five new libraries) we badly wanted to increase the collaborative learning spaces, but lacking ebooks meant much of the space in the libraries had to be used for the print collection. It was frustrating because culturally the students wanted to work and study in groups, wanted to help each other. Had PDA been an option at the time, we could have foregone the expense of steel and paper to house the collection and focused on better space utilization, adapted to the ways the students liked to study.

As we started searching for ebook options, we were continually frustrated. Increasingly, the only ebooks available were from vendors that sold them in "packages." The problem was that we needed books on the geosciences, but to get them had to purchase a "science" package that included material dealing with medicine. Areas like anatomy could cause considerable problems with the more culturally traditional members of the administration. The politically sensitive content combined with the high price of a package that included more of what we did not want than what we needed made it a deal-breaker; we just could not take a chance on acquiring that kind of blanket offering. Cost was not the real issue because we could easily have afforded a package of the right material.

Another area where PDA would have helped was in the way the material was presented to the students. Building a library in a non-library culture means you spend a great deal of time educating the users about what a library is and how it is organized. Students do not care about a Library of Congress Classification system or a Dewey system; they just want to easily find the information they need without learning a cataloguing system. With the ebook option, we could easily have set up things so they could find what they needed by using the library's online catalogue without the need for them to leave their chairs – everything they needed would be right there in front of them. With print, by contrast, students need to go the shelves and try to decipher the method of organization to find the books.

## Azerbaijan Diplomatic Academy
*Rex Steiner*

My most recent endeavor was the building and development of a new library in the Caucasus on the banks of the Caspian Sea. The library is part of a high-profile institution whose mission is international affairs, diplomacy, and business management. This library's core collection is an assemblage of titles obtained from close examination of North American universities covering the same subjects. A collection of 10,000 items was carefully built and 90 percent of them were acquired. This print collection was housed in a temporary facility while the new campus was under construction.

The desire of the university was to be competitive on a world-wide scale and to develop the library along North American guidelines. The movement is away from warehousing books, with an emphasis on the library as a learning space. Paper and shelves exist but are not the modern library's focus. Creating spaces that the user can tailor to their learning style is the main goal of many new (and newly refurbished) libraries.[2] For a new university in the Caucasus, where distance is a huge barrier, the opportunity exists to take real advantage of technology and to learn lessons from libraries that are trying to change from the warehouse way of thinking to a more electronic emphasis. ADA has a golden opportunity to break away from being a traditional library and to create a new model as a library that focuses on being able to conform to the user's style of learning.

The complication is that, as is true of several libraries around the Arabian Gulf, administrators want to physically see what they are buying. Ebooks do not take shelves and have no "wow" factor that a library full of print books has. The high profile of this library makes it politically important for government officials and foreign emissaries to find a space that visually impresses. Ebooks have no such political effect.

On the other hand the library requires material that would be politically sensitive, even controversial, in fulfilling its mission. The material might not sit well on shelves with many government visitors, and as a result we were cautious about what made it to the shelves. With an ebook, there is no real danger that a visitor will stumble across a politically sensitive book, making them a good solution to the problem of what to make available. In a sense, ebooks are there, but not "there." In a PDA environment, most books are not owned so that if any need to be taken out of the collection, no financial losses are involved.

On the other hand, in the Caucasus a number of universities have illustrious histories going back at least back to Soviet times. Many of the older generation of administrators and government officials grew up under the Soviet system and are used to a traditional library. The thought of spending hundreds of thousands of dollars on materials you

---

2   For example, the University of Santa Clara Library where all the furniture has wheels and students can arrange things in any order they choose, combined with high-tech media rooms, collaborative study areas with ceiling to floor whiteboard spaces. In libraries such as this, the user is clearly the focus of the structure, not a print collection.

cannot touch or hold in a designated space called a library makes many people anxious. Again, PDA, because the books it makes available are not bought until used, helps to solve the problem. No huge capital outlay is needed for material that people cannot touch.

One of the challenges for the ADA library, as with all new libraries, was the need to have a viable collection from day one. Traditionally, building a viable opening-day collection takes years and for a library of any scale, millions of dollars. With PDA, literally overnight, the library's catalogue could (and did, in fact) go from 10,000 items to over 150,000 items, and at no cost. The library did not need ten years of intense collection-development work on the part of several bibliographers to have access to a collection comparable to a ten-year-old print-based library in North American. Instead of spending on average $75 per book (a low estimate for this part of the world) expending over $11-million ($75 x 150,000) on the books alone, the library spent less than $5,000 and had overnight access for all of its users. Back when the American University of Sharjah began in 1997, this was not even a remote possibility.

This kind of collection development does require some maintenance and vigilance. With the help of a cooperative vendor, a profile needs to be developed to eliminate questionable material. Because we did not yet have an ILS when the collection went live, individual accounts needed to be set up for all authorized users. However, other factors do not require traditional consideration. Copyright matters were minor because the ebooks have rules encrypted into the materials directly and do not rely on the library staff to be vigilant at the photocopier, scanner, or printer. Because such vigilance is unnecessary with ebooks staff can focus on other tasks. Multiple use is valuable because the library has no need to purchase multiple copies. Granted, restrictions exist, but the ebook systems monitor this for the librarians and therefore do not require the manual vigilance that would be required with monitoring paper copies.

## Effects of PDA
*Rex Steiner and Ron Berry*

Now, as new international institutions plan their libraries, the PDA model is having a major effect on the future of the buildings. Unlike the previous libraries where we have worked, the Azerbaijan Diplomatic

Academy, for example, has the option to use ebooks as a key to how it evolves. PDA has affected planning of libraries in the following ways that were not on the radar for consideration in 1997:

*Acquisition of shelving.* According to a recent proposal by a major U.S. shelving supplier it would take over $300,000 for a new library to buy shelves and almost $40,000 for delivery. The estimate did not include assembly.

*Elimination of Customs clearance.* Processing shipments of books through customs can take considerable time, even if extra fees are paid to speed clearance. The result is frustration for the library and its users (not to mention the expense).

*Shipping is expensive and involves risks.* In some parts of the world, not all companies will insure shipments. Library orders can be at risk if there is a traffic accident and the truck with the library's books overturns or the ship delivering the opening-day collection turns out to have been infested by paper-eating insects (yes, it has happened). With the PDA model, there is no risk of shipping delays or in-transit disasters.

*Processing issues.* Even before the print book enters the country, processing services can cause delays. In a small library, it is impossible to do all the processing in house, so we rely on the print book vendor to do such work. Rush orders arrive without processing – which means the library has to process the book by itself. With ebooks, none of this occurs. Having the "right" call number is not an issue; you do not have to do any special physical processing; if the user wants the book, they request it and have immediate access. There is also no risk of mis-shelving the book or of being unable to find the item, perhaps frustrating students who liked to "hide" books in the library so that only they could find them when they wanted them.

*Multiple copies.* With a PDA system that allows simultaneous use, there is no need to buy extra copies; multiple users can access a book as needed. If the book is a key part of a class, the library can purchase it and therefore get more value for the money so that each use will not result in additional charges.

*Preservation.* Special considerations are being undertaken for the care of the print collection, at additional financial cost. However, with ebooks no concern for humidity or mold-growth exists. Because in a PDA environment the library owns very few of the books that are accessible to patrons, concerns about archiving are quite small. Administrators are relieved to know that the e-collection will not be affected physically and that no additional financial resources are needed to secure the collection from external environmental threats.

*Hostile Neighbors.* Issues of security are real in the Middle East and in the Caucasus. Governments concern themselves with the prospect of military threats. Ebooks are, perhaps paradoxically, more secure than print. If national libraries or cultural monuments were destroyed in military conflict, such as the shelling of the Bosnian National Library in Sarajevo in August 1992 or the gutting of the Kuwaiti National Library in the first Gulf War, ebooks would be secure, thousands of miles away. If the library evacuated to a new location, full access would be achievable quickly, without attempting to move huge numbers of print volumes during an emergency, at great human and financial risk.

*Rethinking Library Spaces.* With the elimination of large numbers of shelf units, the library gains floor space. The big question becomes, "What do we do with all this space?" Answering that question means finding a way to use the space so that the library's patrons feel comfortable and can study according to their needs. The savings that PDA brings to the library make it possible to buy mobile furniture that allows students to move into configurations that they like. Money can be re-purposed to media rooms where students can learn and collaborate with others to develop presentations and create projects with the most current technology. Additional study rooms are also a consideration. For ADA, none of these options would have been affordable under the older building models. PDA created an immediate comprehensive collection and then the wherewithal to try new things and develop a more proactive approach to supporting users.

*How much to budget.* In a start-up library, one of the most important aspects of PDA is how to budget for it. The first year is the most difficult. Because the library is new, it has no hard data of its own upon which to base a budget. Not until after the first year, when information literacy classes are held and a more concentrated integration within the curriculum focusing on ebooks takes effect will it become easier to plan the budget. Judging how much the library's financially valuable print collection will be accessed is difficult because it is not known which volumes will actually be used. Access to the PDA collection of over 150,000 volumes, will be much easier to budget in the future because we can track exactly what has been used and how much we spent. Even though there may be some challenges to budgeting, it is certain that access to the 150,000 PDA volumes will cost less than the initial outlay for an opening-day collection of nearly 10,000 print volumes. In the end, the institution saves tens of thousands of dollars using the PDA model.

*Having a back-up plan.* One way of trying to cover the budget and not run out of money is to integrate ebook access into the library's print book budget. Book vendors are willing to incorporate short-term loans and ebook purchases into their supply agreements. Ultimately, it is best to have one budget for acquisitions of either print or ebooks, but at one library the administration requested us to keep the budgets separate. The library uses print as a last resort.

*Balancing print and ebook purchases.* Some faculty and some administrators continue to have a print-first purchasing priority. They hold firm to the concept that a core collection in a discipline must be print, and their thinking has its own validity We believe, however, that a well-managed collection-development strategy in the second decade of the Twenty-first Century uses many formats and modes of access for materials. If an institution insists on print first, a collection of PDA titles is a viable option in providing greatly extended coverage around a core print collection while providing flexible pricing options for materials that may or may not see actual use. While not everything is available electronically much is. For users who want paper, and they are the most vocal, we simply obtain paper.

*Faculty recruitment.* For many institutions in the developing world recruiting faculty is an ongoing challenge. One of the concerns consistently raised by faculty is the seeming geographic isolation from their peer networks which could jeopardize their ability to continue scholarship. Access to appropriate library materials is critical to allay these concerns. To support requests for print books, libraries generally use the following as best-case scenarios: some form of resource sharing with a parent institution with international courier service that would enable a three- to four-day delivery; a rush order account with an online book vendor such as Amazon or Barnes and Noble with expedited international shipping, allowing seven- to ten-day delivery; and finally, ordering through an established academic print book vendor, which usually takes six to eight weeks. All three of these options reassure faculty, *and* they incur enormous additional costs to the library. The PDA model eliminates or greatly reduces these financial burdens.

*Lack of resource sharing in the region.* New international libraries such as the ADA tend not to have established resource-sharing networks in place at their inception. As a result, providing dependable inter-library loan (ILL) can be challenging and expensive, likely leading to frustration from both the library's perspective and to the end user. In much of the developing world there just simply is not a tradition of ILL.

*New programs.* As the plan for the ADA evolves, so does the academic offering. As is normal with young institutions, the programs change and are modified regularly and at times without notice to the library. As a result, the library must be very responsive to shifting needs of the institution and integrate new expectations into the collection-development strategies. Given the inherent challenges of building core print collections quickly, having what essentially can be called a pre-populated collection of PDA titles can quickly serve the needs of students and faculty of the new programs.

*Future Trends.* Concerns are raised by administration about which format is really going to be the "standard." They worry that a new format will arise and make the ebooks currently accessible by the library obsolete. The PDA method, of course, enables the library to stay dynamic and keep up with changes at little financial risk. If a dramatic change in format occurred, then the ebooks available through PDA would change as quickly as the market dictates. But while we have access to 150,000 volumes, we have not purchased them – therefore, we cannot be "stuck" with an obsolete format. In fact, using PDA allows us to keep using the most up-to-date formats available, something that may not be an option if we purchased the ebooks outright and then discovered in a few years that they were no longer readable.

In the future, academic libraries need to find a way to balance these claims: the paper-first group; the electronic preferred; the old-guard traditionalists; and those who simply want information, in whatever format possible. In today's library world, the balance is not easy. What is practical to one group is sacrilege to the other. All of the groups vie for political influence in the development of the library. Often in a start-up library in the developing world, the university librarian does not have the final say; the provost, chancellor, benefactor, or head of state decides. Librarians can be caught in the middle, trying to find ground that satisfies each group as much as possible. It is not an easy task, but it is an exciting one in this world of modern librarianship.

Patron-driven acquisitions – or use-driven acquisitions, as we like to call it – gives the international librarian the ability to gain access to huge numbers of electronic resources at minimal economic risk. Because we pay only for what is actually used, money is not wasted on print books that may never leave their expensive shelves. A book is needed, so it is accessed – no guesswork required and no questions from administrators as to why money was spent on such an item. In the international library world, anxiety by benefactors is high about allowing a librarian to manage what is often the largest departmental budget in the institution. We explain that libraries have managed these resources for centuries and have standards in place to guide us, but the nervousness is real. In the end, the administration wants to be certain it is spending money on materials that they want and need for progress of the institution, and they want to know they are placing their trust and resources in the right person. Really two issues are at work, investing in the information resources, and investing trust in the library staff. PDA helps librarians to ease the stress of some administrators because the financial risk is comparatively low, with almost no money spent on things that may not be used.

PDA allows libraries to get books into the hands of more users that normally would not go out of their way to find an ebook. With proper integration into the library's online catalogue, ebooks become more and more popular. No longer do users need to scribble-down the call number, get-up, go to the shelves, try and decipher the classification system, and hope they can find the book. For most this is an exercise in frustration and rarely ends in success. With ebooks, by contrast, everything is in front of them. The ease of use and the breadth and depth of the e-collection means that a new international library can immediately compete with the old-style libraries in North America or Europe in its holdings of current content. In home-grown institutions in the developing world, this can be a critical selling-point: "Our library has access to as many new volumes as many of the top libraries in North America."

## Summary

During the past ten years, we have been privileged to be involved with the evolution of international libraries in a locally created and operated environment. We have been involved in setting up paper-focused librar-ies and have helped sort through the bureaucracy to make those collections a reality. Early on, we helped create a library that wanted to focus on ebooks but could not find the content. Today, no longer is paper-first a necessity of collection development. Down the years, the expense of building a collection based on print volumes has not changed greatly; it remains a costly method of developing a new library. But, today the flexibility of PDA makes building a collection with great breadth and depth very easy, and it can be done at little financial risk. The benefits of this method far outweigh any negatives. Using PDA as a collection tool means libraries have the flexibility to give users what they want and need. A new library today can start out as a cutting-edge, learning-centered institution with a premium collection in a very short time; it does not need ten years or more to develop a useful academic collection. Today, libraries should be evaluated based on how many people are in them using innovative spaces to create knowledge. A library full of books and no people is no longer a symbol of how good a library is – it is a symbol of how the modern library should not be.

# Chapter 6
# Patron-Driven Acquisitions in School Libraries:
# The Promise and the Problems

Tom Corbett

*Cushing Academy, Ashburnham, Massachusetts*

Cushing Academy's[1] decision in 2009 to move toward a "bookless" library created a stir both inside and outside the library profession. A front-page article from the *Boston Globe*, with a photograph of the Academy's headmaster, Dr. James Tracy, standing amid broken down bookshelves and scratching his head, conveyed an impression of trepidation and doubt (Boston.com 2011). In reality the decision was made both confidently and strategically as part of the Academy's long-range plan to build a "Twenty-first Century Leadership" curriculum.

The Academy was committed to finding better ways to deliver school library services in the "Digital Age." Besides improving access to subscription databases, connecting students and faculty to quality free web sites and datasets, and helping to organize and teach the digital tools used on campus, the library was also charged with delivering digital book-length materials to students and faculty. This last charge, while very much in keeping with a library's traditional role of lending books, was paradoxically the most difficult, especially considering that the goal was to *improve* library services, not disable, debilitate, or philistinize them, as many commentators suggested.

Digital delivery of long-form reading potentially has many advantages over the paper-based alternative, the most obvious being efficient storage, improved inventory control, and 24/7 access. However, other less obvious but equally important advantages include opportunities to provide access to a much larger collection of books than previously possible and to empower patrons with a more direct role in collection development. At the heart of these improvements is patron-driven

---

1  Cushing Academy is a private co-educational day and boarding school in Ashburnham, Massachusetts, United States, for students in grades 9 through 12.

acquisitions, a model potentially as important for school libraries as it is for other types of libraries. Indeed, the benefits of PDA are perhaps even greater in secondary education than at the college level, since school libraries are asked to provide research resources covering a wide range of academic topics, but with smaller book budgets than their academic counterparts. While the number of students served by the school library may be smaller, the range of core academic topics remains roughly the same. In the age of paper-based books, this required careful collection development and considerable compromise. In 2010 the median high school book budget was around $12,000, allowing for roughly 400 titles to be added each year (Farmer 2011). The typical 14,000 volume book collections are obviously inadequate for serious research, but, until now, they were all that was possible.

Digital delivery greatly expands options, but only if libraries, publishers, and vendors think beyond the business models of the past. Simply overlaying one-to-one lending and print ownership on top of a set of digital resources does little to expand a school library's collection. Digital books may reduce the need for floor space and increase access to titles after hours (if, going by traditional approaches, the books are not already checked out), but school libraries are still left with the same limitations on collection size and patron empowerment as before. At Cushing Academy, digitizing the *status quo* was not acceptable. We wanted to show how shifting to digital resources could benefit our students and faculty enough to make the drastic change of radically reducing our print collection worthwhile.

## Two Primary Roles for the School Library

Before reviewing how we have implemented and benefited from PDA at Cushing Academy, it is important to consider the two, fairly distinct, though related roles for our school library. One role is to support long-form reading, often for pleasure and not tied specifically to the class curriculum. As a boarding school, we feel an added responsibility to shape student habits and interests and provide resources that may go beyond what is typical in a day school. Like all educators, we want students who come to the school as readers, to stay readers; of course, we also want to entice non-readers to become readers. We feel strongly that immersive, long-form reading should remain vital in the Twenty-first Century and that its prospects and importance will be enhanced through a digital approach. To support this reading role, we primarily use Kindles and Amazon ebook content. While the technology and choice of vendor do not readily lend themselves to a PDA approach, we feel we have moved the service in the direction of PDA as well as the technology allows.

The other important role for our secondary school library is to support research and information literacy. This role *is* closely tied to the curriculum and access to monographs is delivered primarily through EBL to our student's laptop and other multimedia devices. Typically the research service is associated more with database and web research, and, at the high-school level, does not often result in cover-to-cover, long-form reading. Nonetheless, important content resides in monographic works that high-school students should be exposed to and utilize, albeit more at the chapter and section level. This research role benefits greatly from a PDA approach as its value is partly proportional to the size and breadth of the collection being searched. As we have discovered at Cushing, PDA expands the number of nonfiction monographs our students have access to from less than 20,000 to nearly 200,000 titles.

## Amazon Kindles and PDA

At first glance, it is hard to see how Amazon Kindles and ebooks can fit with a PDA approach. As of early 2011, Amazon has provided no library services or offered any kind of serious lending support for the digital content it sells. Based on its own proprietary Digital Rights Management (DRM) platform, a Kindle will not work with existing library lending platforms that rely on the Adobe DRM model. Kindle users are out of luck if they want to borrow materials from vendors such as Overdrive or even EBL.

Despite this serious limitation, Kindles and ebooks purchased from Amazon have worked well in service of the library's reading support role. For one, Kindles are an excellent long-form reading device, with e-ink display and state-of-the-art functionality, such as text-to-speech and a well integrated dictionary. Just as important, the Amazon DRM allows an unlimited number of devices to be joined to one account and permits up to six copies of one title to be shared among six of those devices. Perhaps most important, the popular, best-selling content available through Amazon supports the recreational reading interests of our students and faculty.

In what way can the Amazon approach be used in patron-driven acquisition? At Cushing, we find the speed at which requested titles can be purchased and loaded on to the next available Kindle, or delivered electronically to a Kindle already checked out, works well. The nearly instantaneous, although mediated, process allows us to respond to patron demand without pre-purchasing the content. Moreover, we can instantly buy additional copies to accommodate our 7$^{th}$, 13$^{th}$ and 19$^{th}$ readers of a particularly popular title. Nearly all of the more than 1,000 titles we have purchased over the past two years have been a direct result of student and faculty requests. We know each title has been read at least once, and most many more times than that.

The true advantage, however, lies in this: our students have nearly immediate access to more than one million titles. With so many choices we can encourage students to select titles based more on their interests than simply on what we own. We direct them to sources such *Novelist Plus* and *Gale's Books and Authors* to explore genres and find similar authors (see image 1). Titles found on those services link out to Amazon for availability and further review, not our catalogue. While it is true that some titles are not available as ebooks, most newer and popular titles are, resulting in a selection far greater and more current than could ever be found on a library shelf. What is more, by directing students to these sites, they are exposed to a large and dynamic culture of readers, encouraging them to read reviews and connect with authors.

Most importantly, students have responded. Since early 2010, over 1,000 Kindle ebooks have been purchased, based almost entirely on requests. All 90+ Kindle e-readers are checked out and new units are purchased every semester to avoid waiting lists. Our users are encouraged to keep the e-reader for the semester if they continue to read, with requested titles purchased by the library often delivered electronically to their borrowed units. Students and faculty appreciate the serendipity of finding other books already on the device besides the titles requested. Users also tell us they use the embedded dictionary frequently; and our ESL students especially like the text-to-speech feature, often preferring the slow mechanical voice to the peculiar New England accents around them. Clearly, recreational, long-form reading can thrive in the digital age, even among digital-natives.

Home » Fiction

**Fantasy**

## What is Fantasy fiction?

"With its intuitive, rather than rational, approach, *Fantasy fiction* describes a world that never could exist, one where magic rules. *Fantasy fiction* deals more with emotions and relationships than ideas, and *Fantasy* cherishes and preserves familiar stories, legends, and myths, retelling them, sometimes with a twist. These are often elegantly written stories with a haunting quality, with something just behind the story, something bigger than the story itself that hints at a larger meaning." (Description from *Novelist Plus*.)

Explore this genre at: Books and Authors or Novelist Plus

| Title▲ | Description | Added |
| --- | --- | --- |
| Airborn | Matt, a young cabin boy aboard an airship, and Kate, a wealthy young girl traveling with her chaperone, team up to search for the existence of mysterious winged creatures reportedly living hundreds of feet above the Earth's surface | 2010-09 |
| The amber spyglass | Lyra and Will find themselves at the center of a battle between the forces of the Authority and those gathered by Lyra's father, Lord Asriel | 2010-09 |

Image 1: http://fwlibrary.cushing.org/taxonomy/
term/14414

## Ebook Library and PDA

While we think our Amazon model is a better approach for supporting reading than the earlier paper-based models, it is obviously far from perfect. It requires considerable staff mediation and a purchase-only option for collection development. At the end of the day, libraries are still left with more purchased content than they might like. That is, the equivalent of multiple copies of books sit unused on electronic shelves long after their popularity and prime value passes. For research purposes, the content on the Kindles is mostly locked away, now in their digital containers, and typically only findable through metadata indexing, such as a MARC record.

EBL's PDA and non-linear lending business models offer a much more sophisticated approach that can greatly benefit school libraries. Theirs is the long-term business model we are hoping to move to entirely in support of both library roles, but for now we rely on it mostly to facilitate our research and information literacy services.

Consider the traditional role of the paper-based, nonfiction book collection in school libraries. Such collections stood apart from library databases, accessible only through physical browsing or the minimal metadata indexing of the library's integrated library system. In contrast, ebook collections can have their entire full-text content tightly integrated into one federated search that includes both databases and ebooks. At Cushing Academy we have partnered with Deep Web Technologies to implement their best-of-class federated search service with this important goal of integrating ebook and database content in mind. In fact, this federated search is now the primary search tool for accessing the content the library provides in support of research and information discovery. It has replaced our ILS-based OPAC, which, after all, was a discovery tool for mostly what a library owns, not the larger collection of information the library provides access to.

This leads to another important aspect of PDA: the ebooks do not have to be owned by the library in order to be made available for research. Instead, in a PDA construction, they exist ready for purchase or rental at the moment they are pulled from the federated search result set and identified as worthwhile by the student. At Cushing, we call this a *research-driven acquisition* model that elevates the status and accessibility of monographic content with that of full-text journals and databases. Far from signaling the end of monographs in the school library by their removal from rarely visited stacks, digital PDA models such as EBL's can potentially increase the accessibility and value of their digital equivalents for years to come. In a manner similar to the full-text indexing of Google Books, this approach can unlock monograph content previously hidden, but, unlike Google Books, make it immediately accessible in a library environment. In the age of *"the long tail,"* with approaches such as PDA, libraries do not need to own the copy-righted tail to give immediate access to much of its length.

How is it possible to provide access to significantly more ebooks in school libraries given that typically tight, even shrinking, budgets prevail? First, purchases made from demonstrated demand can be appealing to funders, possibly attracting additional funding. Second, digital lending through EBL offers a rental option allowing libraries to pay less for resources of limited appeal and short-lived usefulness. Third, non-linear lending, which allows multiple simultaneous use of books, is a far more efficient means of managing titles that are in brief demand but where usage tails off dramatically. Fewer copies need to be purchased to meet initial high demand and fewer copies need to be weeded after demand expires. This all helps to stretch the same acquisition dollars over a much larger collection of resources by more efficiently tying costs to actual use.

## Collection Development and PDA

One common criticism of PDA made by school librarians is that this model appears to take away the librarian's collection development responsibilities, a traditionally important facet of school librarianship (Gray 2009). Perhaps owing to the limitations of a small collection supporting a broad curriculum, school librarians have had to pick titles carefully and make every dollar count. However, it is not necessarily a bad outcome to loosen some of this control and empower students and faculty with more of a say in the process. In many ways this brings library services closer to the new Twenty-first Century educational paradigm. That said, PDA does not preclude librarians from continuing to play an important role in the selection of material. In a digital PDA environment, the library does not need to own an item before recom-mending it to users. If title recommendations are good ones, that is, if students or faculty respond to the choices, then they are purchased upon request. In an EBL model, the purchase (or rental) can be transparent to the user, looking as if the title has been owned all along; in the Amazon model the process is more mediated, but the title is potentially delivered to the user's device within minutes.

At Cushing Academy we are using multiple methods to direct our users to recommended ebooks, whether already owned or not. Our library's home page, along with overhead LCD screens in the library,

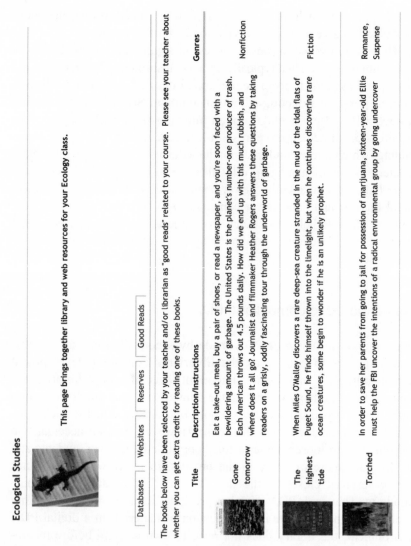

Image 2: http://fwlibrary.cushing.org/courses/science/ecological_studies
(open the tab for "Good Reads")

highlight new ebook titles to catch the eyes of students and faculty. Moreover, each course taught at Cushing Academy has its own dedicated library page, highlighting databases, web resources, *and individual ebooks* deemed appropriate for that class. Nonfiction titles are linked within the "Reserves" tab; fiction and popular nonfiction titles that complement the course subjects are linked within the "Good Reads" tab (see image 2).

These titles may or may not be already owned by the library; and it does not really matter. They will be purchased or borrowed once a student clicks on the link and finds the ebook useful (EBL titles) or contacts the library to arrange for an extra-credit book report (Amazon titles).

Another way librarians can affect the proper selection of titles in a research-driven acquisitions process is by teaching the student how to best identify appropriate ebook content within their search results. Indeed, learning how to differentiate the wheat from the chaff within a set of results is an essential Twenty-first Century information literacy skill and one that librarians should see as essentially a collection development task in a PDA environment. Skilled students not only make for better researchers, but also better library collections.

## Challenges

In the long run the library should not be in the device business, whether the devices are paper, e-readers, or multimedia tablets. Our focus should be on content freed from any particular device, connecting our users to the ideas, insights and imagined worlds of content creators. Unfortunately, the PDA model, and its close cousins just-in-time (JIT) inventory management and non-linear lending, are currently tied to particular technologies, primarily due to the need for digital rights management (DRM). Three or more DRM models compete in the current marketplace, with each vendor keen on using its technology to lock out competitors and increase market share. Making matters worse is that many publishers only work with specific vendors, thereby locking their content into only one DRM format or another. The market situation makes acquisitions and content delivery difficult for libraries and their users, limiting the overall value of a digital approach. We have hope, however, that as publishers, vendors, libraries, and end-users become more fully engaged with digital lending, the market will motivate the process to become less device-dependent and more user focused.

Another current challenge impeding the adoption of PDA within school libraries is the lack of age-appropriate content from vendors such as EBL. The lack is not surprising since to this point the academic market has been much more interested in PDA than school libraries. However, as additional school libraries become aware of PDA and create more demand, vendors may be able to seek out and attract publishers of age-appropriate material. Attracting these publishers should also reduce the average costs of individual titles in the PDA databases as school-appropriate materials are typically priced significantly lower than academic titles. Given the financial restraints that require school libraries to choose the titles they now buy almost surgically, a PDA model that allows rental will enable many more books to find their way to discovery by existing as choices rather than as purchases.

However, since publishers benefit from many of the flaws in the current library business model – too many copies of books on shelves (whether electronic or steel) represent sales, not inefficiency – it is by no means a given that they will readily see the advantages of PDA and non-linear lending. It is up to librarians to insist that a shift to digital resources must *improve* library services while still protecting the economic value of what publishers have to sell.

In the end, the most serious challenge to the adoption of PDA in the school market may simply be the viability of monographic resources themselves. Book-length nonfiction may no longer be in demand by faculty and, by extension, students within the Twenty-first Century classroom. With a shift toward project-based learning and e-textbooks linking out to shorter-length web (and, we hope, library) resources, the value of monographs, especially nonfiction titles in direct support of the curriculum, may be greatly diminished. Monographs may be just too linear for the modern classroom. Despite our early success, long-form fiction may also be less in demand as digital-natives continue to be pulled in so many directions and enticed by myriad information and entertainment choices. These challenges are, of course, not a criticism of PDA itself but simply a shift in the types of resources used inside and outside of the classroom, independent of how they are acquired and delivered.

Then again, there may be a timeless value to long-form reading and the careful, analytical and immersive qualities it embodies. There may also be new forms of monographs, not quite so linear, that will want to be shared in a school environment. If so, PDA offers the best method for making those resources economically viable in a school library for both content creators and users. It also allows students and faculty to become more empowered and connected with the development of their shared library resources. It helps the school library remain viable in the Twenty-first Century.

# References

"A library without the books - The Boston Globe." Boston.com - Boston, MA news, breaking news, sports, video. 31 Mar. 2011 (Boston.com 2011).

Anderson, Chris. *The Long Tail: Why the Future of Business Is Selling Less of More*. New York: Hyperion, 2006. Kindle Electronic Book.

Bonk, Curtis J. "How Technology Is Changing School." *Educational Leadership* 67, no. 7 (April 2010): 60–65. (As Summarized in Effective Schools Research Abstracts Volume 25, Issue 1.)

Corbett, Thomas B. "The Changing Role of the School Library's Physical Space." *School Library Monthly*. 31 March 2011 <http://www.schoollibrary monthly.com/articles/Corbett2011-v27n7p5.html>.

Farmer, Lesley. "SLJ's Spending Survey: As the Economy Limps along and Federal Dollars Dwindle, School Librarians Are Turning into Resourceful Survivors." *Library Journal: Library News, Reviews and Views*. Web. 06 Apr. 2011. <http://www.libraryjournal.com/slj/articlessurveys/889109-351/sljs_spending_survey_as_the.html.csp>.

Gray, Liz, Cheryl Steele, and Cassandra Barnett. "Technology and the Printed Page Are Not Mutually Exclusive." *School Library Journal* 55, no. 11 (November 2009): 10-11. Advanced Placement Source, EBSCOhost (accessed November 20, 2010).

# Chapter 7
# PDA and Publishers

David Swords

*Ebook Library*

This chapter has been a bear. Our first idea was to ask a publisher to write from the publisher's point of view about PDA. Maybe we did not ask the right publisher, maybe the assignment was too burdensome or too fraught, but we had no takers. Then we thought it best to interview different publishers, and some were willing to talk and had a lot of valuable things to say.[1] Some publishers have focused on PDA and are carrying out experiments of their own; others shun it. It became clear that looking from the outside, a kind of environmental scan, might prove more useful than a debate among the converted, the interested skeptics, and the doubters within publishing. Ultimately, the main audience for this chapter is publishers, at best those who so far have rejected, discounted, or feared PDA. It was with them in mind that we went to Mike Shatzkin, a consultant, owner of the Idea Logical Company, whose work is familiar to almost anyone in trade publishing or book retailing and who has thought longer and harder than anyone I know about the effects of ebooks on the world of publishing.[2] Shatzkin is not expert on academic libraries and had never heard of PDA before we talked. But he grasped the concept immediately.

---

1    In particular, thanks to Hannah Perrett of Cambridge University Press and to Katrin Siems of Walter de Gruyter for their insights.

2    Shatzkin is the founder and CEO of The Idea Logical Company, which counts among its customers the Book Industry Study Group, the Digital Book World Conference, Ingram, and many others. Shatzkin's blog, *The Shatzkin Files*, is always worth reading and can be found at http://www. idealog.com/blog/.

## The Eye of the Needle

Shatzkin's first comment pretty much summed up the situation in which publishers and libraries find themselves. He asked rhetorically whether anyone in our corner of the world does not realize that budgets, perhaps *especially* book budgets, are shrinking, that shelf space is at a premium. He said, "The eye of the needle is getting clogged. The question of how the pain of less money chasing more books will be distributed is open. But there is no question that there will be pain." Overall libraries are buying less now and chances are their budgets will not grow next year or the year after that. "Ultimately," he said, "the old model for how libraries buy their books will break down and go away."

We can follow Mike's idea along a slightly different path by pointing out the proliferation of information available to people, and that for libraries to remain useful they need to enable access to many of those resources. Doing so has costs. It seems unlikely that libraries can sustain buying a high percentage of books that are not used or used only lightly when so many resources that will be used clamor for their dollars. Publishers can choose not to accept the situation, can believe that their house will rise above it, or they can look for another way. We hear from publishers that the present acquisitions model is predictable; they worry that PDA will be unpredictable and that revenues will drop. Against that is the certainty of reduced spending on books by libraries.

During the 2008 recession budgets in many libraries around the world crumbled. As universities faced the prospect of layoffs and as basic services appeared imperiled, books began to look like a luxury. Administrators canceled book budgets and saw that the library did not languish for want of them. In the aftermath of the recession some administrators demanded that libraries make do with smaller budgets. Whether it is coincidence or causally related, at that point many libraries began to take PDA seriously. For a library director, PDA meant the ability to go to a dean or provost and say that less money could deliver more books. The argument was compelling. Several chapters in this book cite research showing that the speculative methods, such as approval plans, that libraries have used to buy monographs until now lead to a preponderance of unused or barely used tomes lining their shelves. Their mere presence has costs, never mind the price of the book. As academic administrators consider their budgets, the speculative approach is likely to chase library money to more used resources, ones in which book publishers may play no part. PDA, on the other hand, because it might be a means of giving any library access to more books than ever before, to a collection that need not grow old, and most of all to spend scarce money only on what is clearly needed by patrons, could prove a viable alternative.

In Chapter 3, Michael Levine-Clark shows that as books age in a library they are used less. Shatzkin put the idea slightly differently, saying that each year a smaller percentage of a traditional library collection is valuable. The collection almost inevitably and invariably gets older even if budgets grow. The data suggesting that the relatively small percentage of books a library can afford to buy from what is available indicate not that selectors make poor choices. Instead, their role is like wagering on a horse race. They bet the odds based on what can be known from history, and as is true of the best handicappers, will be wrong most of the time. If over the years statistics time and again show that 80 percent of the books a library buys will be used so little as to represent a poor investment by any financial measure, then at some point the pressure to use money to more valuable ends will drive all but the most inveterate gamblers to healthier professions. That is, if speculative buying of books continues, the statistics libraries cite to justify their trials of PDA, another way to use and acquire books, will at some point become statistics administrators use either to slash budgets or to insist that money be spent on anything but books.

Longstanding acquisitions models have made academic libraries warehouses for publishers. In the retail business, Shatzkin says, bookstores order what they think they need and return what they cannot sell. As a result inventory has been a huge problem for publishers. When returns start coming, profitable books suddenly become losers. In the academic market print runs for scholarly books are small. Libraries are habituated to buying books when they appear fearing that ones they want will be out of print if they wait. But buying a book when it is first out means buying when least is known about it. The book has not been reviewed, has not been cited. And if it turns out to sit unused on the shelf, unlike a bookstore, a library cannot return it. In short, in the academic library market the problem of unsold, or unused stock shifts from the publisher to the library. To a great degree it is the library that risks its coin.

PDA, a phenomenon of ebooks, puts neither party at risk of uneconomical warehousing. Publishers have no printing and no returns. Libraries need not serve as warehouses whose shelves are stocked with material that cannot be returned once the likelihood that it will be needed by library consumers diminishes. Rather than mostly old and relentlessly aging inventory, the library can continually weed old ebooks no one has used and replace them with new books someone might want. Or, perhaps the library will not weed them at all.

## "Chunkable" Content

Mike is one of those rare people who throws off ideas like sparks from a steel blade on a grindstone. In talking about PDA and academic libraries, he was outside his normal retail element, and I did not immediately understand when he said, "As a publisher my resistance to PDA is proportional to how 'chunkable' my content is. If it is chunkable I am more nervous. If I deliver a cookbook and all the reader wants is a recipe for veal parmesan then a lot of people will be satisfied without any money changing hands."

The browse period that some aggregators allow, ebrary and EBL at this writing, is long enough that, in fact, many patrons find what they need before the library pays for them to use the book. And Mike pointed out that the matter goes deeper. Most of the people using academic libraries are undergraduates or even graduate students looking to do research to fulfill an assignment or to learn something fairly specific that concerns a class they are taking. Few of these patrons are likely to read the books they scan or borrow. Much more often they mine the books. EBL data show that a fair percentage of the time data mining occurs within the five-minute browse window the company allows for books a library does not own. And when this happens, the publisher makes nothing.

At this point in the conversation my heart began to chunk. Mike seemed to be saying that under the conditions that prevail at academic libraries, where "chunking" as opposed to reading is pretty much what happens with most monographs, a PDA model would be disastrous for publishers. The free browse was bad enough. But even if the patron wanted a loan, the library could rent the book at a fraction of the cost of buying it. For publishers to allow such practice seemed nothing but folly. Mike, however, has the ability to see beyond the obvious.

All of us who were serious students recall that most of the time our research in the college library was hostage to what the library contained, and even then, the best books always seemed to be checked out to someone else. If books we wanted were not in the library we usually made do with the books that were. For publishers this means that most libraries most of the time will lack most of their books, a budgetary fact of life. Students make do with what happens to be on the local shelf or perhaps on the shelf of a nearby library. For a publisher, if your book is not on the shelf, it cannot be discovered, cannot be cited, cannot yield revenue. But if your books can be on the virtual shelves of hundreds of libraries because they do not have to be bought to arrive there in the first place, then their chances of being found and cited rise exponentially. In a world where discovery is often, if not mainly, through the library, PDA becomes both a sales and a marketing channel.

## Competing for Eyeballs

In traditional acquisitions models if a library does not buy a book when it is new, chances are it will never buy the book. In North America or Australia, the eyes of one selector fall upon one slip one time, and if the scant data on a new book fail to deliver a purchase on the spot, the book almost always disappears forever from notice. PDA, by contrast, puts a record in a catalogue, usually for years, where it has the chance to attract notice from the hundreds or thousands of eyes that use the catalogue as their discovery tool. The situation is Darwinian; the odds of survival, or of sales, improve with numbers. A few books on a few shelves, as happens for most publishers under current acquisitions models for academic libraries, may be enough to make a book successful in that channel. But the statistical odds that a book will succeed over the long term, both economically and as a research tool, rise massively if it is on hundreds of shelves over many years. With books, a citation here can lead to notice there. The more virtual shelves upon which a book can reside, the more eyes that can find it, and the better the chance that casual, temporary interest by one student can lead to broader, more serious interest. Mike made the point that if most books are used more when they are new, world events – an oil spill or an earthquake – can suddenly make old books important. The long tail that PDA offers gives books a library would not have bought the chance to be found and used when events deliver them from obscurity.

Mike has written in his blog many times about the direction of book pricing and the ways in which publishers can make up in numbers what they lose in average transaction amounts. A numerical way to consider the situation is that libraries with full-blown PDA programs on average spend about \$15 to \$23 per transaction,[3] depending on various factors, a number composed of short-term loans and purchases of books that have shown they will be used. Libraries that simply buy outright average about \$75 to \$105 per transaction. If two such libraries have the same budget, let us say \$100,000, the typical PDA library will have almost 6,000 transactions for its \$100,000. The library that buys books outright will have slightly more than 1,100 transactions. The PDA library and its patrons benefit in that almost 5,000 more times someone finds a useful monograph. But the difference is deceiving. First, in the traditional library, many of the books bought will never be used; in the PDA library every expenditure requires a use. The traditional library will buy and put 1,100 books on its shelf and it is to those 1,100 that patrons must look for their research. A PDA library that spends \$100,000, depending on factors such as the number of patrons who use library resources, can make tens of thousands of books available to its patrons, multiplying the likelihood that people will find books they need many times over.

How do publishers benefit? The obvious point is that the odds of their books being included among 50,000, 100,000, or 150,000 are 50, 100, or 150 times higher than the odds of their books being among 1,100. Stay out of PDA and your books will not be available to be cited in dozens of libraries where they might be. Stay clear of PDA and chances are that in most libraries, most of the time, and in increasing numbers as budgets flee or diminish, your books will not be on the virtual shelves. A publisher, Shatzkin points out, cannot win by staying out of PDA unless they can beat the odds that their books will be bought often enough to overcome the entropy inherent in the direction of today's market. From the point of view of a library patron, if the cupboard is nearly bare too many times, as it might appear when the total choice comes to 1,100, you might stop going to the cupboard.

Even if it sounds Cassandra-like, failing to raise one other specter for publishers to consider, open access, would be remiss. Academics for years have railed against a publishing system that restricts scholarly material to those who can afford it. Although it is commercial and does not allow universal access, PDA is an economically viable way to democratize information. The imprimatur conferred by the name of a

---

3    These and the numbers that follow are based on analysis of thirty-five EBL customers in Australia, Canada, New Zealand, and the United States from December 2009 through December 2010.

solid academic publisher on a scholar's work is valuable. But how much more valuable is that imprimatur, and the scholarship itself, if the book can be easily available to scholars at small and large institutions anywhere rather than in a relative few?

PDA has a retail corollary that Shatzkin raised. In the past as books were going out of stock, and online retailers showed only a couple of copies available, sales of remaining copies were depressed. With the advent of print on demand through Lightning Source, the stock number that typically appears is 100 copies for publishers who come in to the program. It turns out that knowing a hundred copies are available lifts sales 20 percent. When you show only a few copies, orders often are not placed. With 100 copies, orders for 10 often occur. Absence and scarcity depress sales. Presence and apparent abundance lift them.

The possibility of discovery includes other benefits. If your book is on the shelf of 100 libraries chances are that some will buy it, many will rent it. Because discovery is through the library catalogue, PDA serves as a marketing opportunity. Publishers who improve the metadata that drive discovery increase the chances that more eyeballs will fall on their books. Improving metadata that leads to discovery may prove a better investment than putting the money into marketing. For students who need to fulfill an assignment marketing has little value. Shatzkin suggests the possibility that a publisher could reallocate marketing costs to raise the profile of the book in the library catalogue.

## Implementing PDA

Certain publishers can bet that they will beat the odds, that libraries large and small will take the gamble, will buy their books. They could be right, especially over the short term. Even so, good reasons may exist for giving PDA a try.

One cannot always know in a conversation when the direction of an idea takes on a life of its own and its momentum drives out counterpoints. But at some point Shatzkin seemed to shake his head over the telephone and concluded, "I don't see why a publisher would stay out of this. There's nothing to lose. Academic libraries buy new books. Take 500 titles from your backlist or 100 titles and try it. See what happens. You were not going to sell these in the market anyway. But now they can live as marketing opportunities in dozens of library catalogues. Why not start with everything that is one year or two years old and older? Try it for six months. See what you can learn. And don't expect PDA to be the end of things."

PDA as a sales model is ultimately no different from the way books are usually sold, that is, at the point of interest or the point of need. If anything, the approach until now of buying on speculation in service of building a collection and against the day when, just in case, someone might need a book is the anomalous prisoner of print technology. Short print runs of books on esoteric subjects created the supply chain that dominates today, that, and the longstanding notion that libraries house books to preserve them. As the idea that libraries provide access has grown, fueled in its immensity by e-journals, the Internet, and now ebooks, it seems inevitable that good ideas for how libraries with resource constraints (that is, every library) can serve their constituents better would emerge. PDA is no more than one such idea. If Shatzkin is right that publishers can try it with their backlist at virtually no risk, then the question of how to go about doing so remains.

An obvious way is to give some portion of your backlist to ebook aggregators – EBL, ebrary, MyiLibrary, and NetLibrary – and see what happens. The advantage is that a publisher's books can immediately become part of the PDA collection that hundreds of libraries make available to their patrons. It is not as if the books need to be sold; generally records for them can simply go into library catalogues. If they were buying ebooks libraries would de-duplicate against their print. PDA, by contrast, encourages many to duplicate intentionally and with good reason. If a duplicated ebook is used lightly, the library can afford a short-term loan and will usually be happy to pay its price. Libraries are eager to learn which edition patrons prefer. And when the print copy is checked out, their patrons need not go away disappointed. If a publisher considers that much of their backlist can quickly be seen and found in catalogues of hundreds of libraries that will own some of their books but not all and that will duplicate their print, the sales boost could be significant. Today libraries commonly use various sources of second-hand books when patrons ask for a backlist title, a workflow in which publishers play no part. By contrast, if your titles live in the catalogue, librarians need not hunt for a book, the patron can use what they need immediately, and the publisher joins the workflow.

Publishers also could learn from data the aggregators can easily report. What information in MARC records, for example, helps discovery? If libraries do not want some of their books in the catalogue, which ones are they? Or conversely, which do they always want and which are they especially willing to duplicate? No good reason exists as to why publishers cannot insist on meaningful periodic data from aggregators as a condition of doing business. Ebooks attract much richer information than print about the behavior of their readers. How much are the books being used and when? How often are they browsed, loaned, or bought? Once owned by libraries, do they attract use? And if immediate sales of new books decline as libraries abandon their practice of buying new before they become unobtainable, replaced by many books on the same topic that await interest, do the long-term, smaller transactions from dozens of libraries effectively counteract the relatively few sales of books that would in the past have been bought speculatively?

On the other hand, PDA may present an opportunity for at least some publishers to dis-intermediate aggregators. Walter de Gruyter and Cambridge University Press, for example, have their own PDA offerings and can choose what or whether to make all or some of their books available through aggregators. If a library wants the advantage of PDA – with no need to spend money at the front – the price of entry may be to work with the publisher directly. The upside is possible increase in profit by losing the middleman. The downside is the need to build an infrastructure, and the need to sell library by library. The investment in technology, sales, and on the back end, administration, could be considerable.

## Entropy and the Unit of Sale

"You need to make a distinction," Shatzkin concluded, "between the unit of sale and the unit of appreciation. In the music business, the unit of sale was the album, the unit of appreciation, the song. The Internet blew up the business model. Now you buy what you want, not what you don't want. Lots of types of books – cookbooks, travel books, manuals – are challenged by digital change. Books in academic libraries face the same challenge. In the past we aggregated things into single purchasable units because physical requirements demanded it. A next step beyond PDA, or an extension of PDA, could easily be ways that allow patrons, or libraries, to rent by the chapter or the page. If so, at some point, the transaction will not be worth negotiating. It will probably be done under aggregate licenses. It could be passed down to the student level. At the beginning of a semester each student might buy in for $25."

On the larger stage books are fighting for their life. Serious novels compete for our time with serious, and seriously good, television drama, sports, films, and myriad other diversions. In libraries, books compete for student and faculty attention with journals, databases, *Wikipedia*, and the Internet itself. It used to be that tools for discovering information in periodicals were primitive. Books were more open to discovery simply by shelf browsing. Not so today. Something that remains consistent for the average undergraduate, whose searches comprise most of the business most academic libraries do, is that the monographs used tend to be the monographs the library happens to have. Students use interlibrary loan but more of the time will circumscribe their research based on what they can have locally.

PDA is much more than a business model that endangers settled ways of acquisitions. It makes libraries better and democratizes information. Rather than carefully choose among a few books to buy, libraries can add records to their catalogues expansively, paying nothing for books that are not used, a little for books that are used lightly, and buying books that prove necessary for students and faculty. Publishers can ignore the model, can assume that the acquisitions practices developed for print, in which libraries buy on speculation before titles disappear, will continue as before. In the dynamic electronic environment we face, however, betting on the past seems an unlikely way to the future. PDA may prove short-lived as books atomize and transactions become more use-based. Or it could evolve. Either way, as Mike Shatzkin suggests, trying PDA has almost no risks, and considerable room exists for publishers to decide how to participate in the model in ways appropriate to their position in the market.

# Part 3
# Modeling PDA

# Chapter 8
# Patron-driven Business Models:
# History, Today's Landscape, and Opportunities

Sue Polanka
*Wright State University*
and
Emilie Delquié
*Publishers Communication Group*

## Introduction

Purchasing ebooks based on the interests of patrons is a popular new business model, no matter what it is called, whether patron-driven acquisition, demand-driven purchasing, or patron-initiated purchase of books. The model exposes available content to patrons by loading MARC records into the library online catalogue. But a library buys only the content that patrons use. Librarians have taken to the model cautiously, as it brings many challenges and uncertainties. This chapter explores the roots of patron-driven acquisition, surveys the current models offered by aggregators and publishers, discusses several of the benefits and challenges of PDA, and compares features of four ebook-aggregator patron-driven approaches.

## The Evolution of Patron-driven Models

Patron-driven acquisition as an ebook business model between libraries and vendors began in 1999. NetLibrary, the first ebook aggregator was based in Boulder, Colorado, and negotiated the idea for allowing patrons to choose the books libraries acquired with the Colorado Alliance of Research Libraries. The Alliance's collection development team, assisted by George Machovec, Associate Director of the Alliance, and the NetLibrary sales force began the negotiations. The Alliance proposed to NetLibrary an option to buy only the books that patrons read. This was based on knowledge that many print books went unused. Since ebooks

were a new medium, the Alliance wanted to guarantee a sound investment by purchasing only titles that people used. When the dust settled
from the negotiations, patron-driven acquisition was born. Brad Norris
from NetLibrary wrote in the Alliance newsletter shortly after negotiations,
"Since the Alliance has a formal contract with NetLibrary, access to the
system has migrated from a charter mode to a patron-driven purchasing
model" (Norris 1999).

The original plan included a complementary first view of a title and
automatic purchase on the second view. According to Machovec, "the
early version was very crude."[1] NetLibrary would periodically provide
MARC records for all of their titles, which were not numerous, making
the loads manageable. The Alliance would load the records into the
local and union catalogues, allowing for discovery by patrons and
possible purchase.

Upon the second view of a title a purchase occurred, and a monthly
bill went to the Alliance, which divided the cost among consortium members according to an algorithm. The titles purchased in these early years
were for a shared collection. All Alliance members had access to the
content for the price of one copy, but use was limited to one person at a
time. David Waggener, who was a sales representative with NetLibrary
in 1999, says publishers complained about the shared collections, but
found it difficult to be decisive because ebooks were new and generating
revenue.[2]

The Alliance soon realized one weakness of patron-driven acquisition
was that it led to buying more content than any budget could afford. To
avoid buying older content, the Alliance decided to keep only recent
MARC records in the catalogue, with one-year old as the limit. Further,
as ebooks became more numerous and popular, the cost of maintaining
the program escalated, requiring additional intervention. Ultimately the
Alliance resorted to approval plan tactics, limiting MARC record loads
and selecting titles individually by subject, publisher, or price.

As costs escalated, the interest in patron-driven acquisition at the
Colorado Alliance waned, and the number of participating members
dropped from 11 to 5 by 2006. The last straw for the Alliance occurred
when NetLibrary's relationship with publishers changed, requiring the
consortium to buy a minimum of two copies of any title acquired through
patron-driven acquisition. The first shared approach to PDA ended.

---

1   Personal conversation with George Machovec, 2010.
2   Personal conversation with David Waggener, 2010.

## Contemporary Patron-driven Models

In the section that follows we describe the aggregator and publisher platforms and business models that allow PDA. Much of the information comes from interviews with principals of the companies who offer PDA and from our experience with the platforms. As you will see, today's approaches are workable, sophisticated, and evolving.

### NetLibrary and Ebooks on EBSCOhost

Despite its promising beginning, NetLibrary declared bankruptcy in 2002 and was acquired by OCLC; in 2010, EBSCO bought NetLibrary. Today NetLibrary offers over 300,000 titles from nearly 700 publishers. The current patron-driven model, launched in 2009, is supported by EBSCO Publishing, at least until June 2011. The model is derived from the original, triggering a purchase when the full text of a book is accessed for a third time. Ebook titles are purchased for individual libraries using the one-book/one-user model, a limitation that has received much criticism in the library community. NetLibrary's model is available through certain book distribution partners, such as YBP Library Services.

One service that NetLibrary has offered throughout the years is personalized collection development. They have professional librarians on staff to assist with the development of a patron-driven plan. Whether using the collection development service or going alone, libraries have the opportunity to preselect content for inclusion in the patron-driven plan. Criteria such as publisher, subject, and price can be used to limit the MARC records loaded into a library's online catalogue.

eBooks on EBSCO*host* should have launched in July 2011, bringing a variety of new business models and opportunities to NetLibrary content. The NetLibrary ebook and audio book content migrated to the EBSCO*host* platform, and the NetLibrary platform was retired. EBSCO plans to release a richer patron-driven program that allows for different purchase models and upgrade paths for libraries that previously invested in the one-book/one-user model.

While details of the ebooks on EBSCO*host* plan remain undisclosed at this writing (April 2011), Ken Breen, Senior Director, eBook Products, says that libraries can acquire titles via patron-driven acquisition based on four activities: total time spent within the full-text, number of pages viewed within the full-text, printing any portion of a title, or downloading portions of a title. Titles can be purchased using a variety of access options such as unlimited users, three users, or a single user, all set at different price points. Libraries can determine the access type within their profile, automatically purchasing access during patron-driven acquisition transactions. Libraries can opt to create their own profile (by selecting the titles to expose to patrons) or choose to have EBSCO Publishing's collection development group tailor a profile to their exact curricular/collection needs. Additional features are listed in the comparative chart in Table 1. EBSCO is negotiating with publishers for worldwide rights to guarantee international availability for their product.


MyiLibrary

MyiLibrary is Ingram Digital's e-content aggregation platform, offering libraries access to nearly 250,000 ebook titles and adding 5,000 new titles per month from over 18,000. Myilibrary was part of Coutts Information Services before both companies were acquired by Ingram Digital in 2006. Coutts' main service had long been approval plans for print books, but the company started to partner with aggregators as ebooks were becoming increasingly popular. At that point Coutts decided to build its own platform to leverage the existing relationships the company had with publishers. In 2004, Coutts assumed that electronic books would be commercialized with models similar to those of their print counterparts.

However, within 18 months of launch, the University of California in Merced suggested that Myilibrary test a model based on use to help the library with its selection process, since they had a severe shortage of collection-development librarians and selectors. MyiLibrary agreed to load all of its content into the University's catalogue and to let the library pay only for the books that were used. At the time, simply opening any part of a book would constitute a use because of the way the platform was built. The model then evolved quickly as more libraries expressed interest in the approach. As a result, the definition of "a use" was refined. Now, "use" is triggered when someone accesses content within the chapters, giving them ample time to review the bibliographic information, reviews, table of contents, and abstract.

Today, MyiLibrary works closely with librarians to determine the number of books accessible to students and faculty appropriate to the budget established for a PDA program. Generally, until a profile is fine-tuned, it is MyiLibrary's experience that librarians can anticipate $1 will be spent for every $3 made visible in the catalogue. MyiLibrary provides MARC records to the library and turns on access to titles meeting the prescribed parameters. Librarians and MyiLibrary can monitor use monthly; use automatically determines which invoices are sent for ebooks that pass the trigger points. The triggers are negotiated individually with each library, but MyiLibrary requires a minimum guaranteed level of expenditure from every library that signs up for the service. These features and others are listed in the comparative chart, Table 1.

The model is popular in the library market. As Carolyn Morris, former Director of Sales, North America, observed, it is encouraging that 80% of the purchased books are used again, so librarians are increasingly confident with their investment in the model.[3] MyiLibrary has found that libraries with fewer online resources tend to have higher use for the content on this platform. Moving forward, MyiLibrary will refine its offerings to the library market. However, it is clear to them that the model is no longer supplemental in the book acquisition process, and more and more it is being incorporated into approval plans.

## Ebook Library (EBL)

**EBL** (Ebook Library) is Ebook Corporation's platform for academic and corporate libraries worldwide. EBL offers libraries access to more than 190,000 titles from hundreds of academic publishers. EBL launched its demand-driven acquisitions model in 2004 to provide multiple simultaneous access to content and to enable libraries to give access to what users need rather than rely on speculative buying. Early on, publishers – particularly in the UK – were interested in testing the approach and librarians – particularly in Australia – were eager to test the model.

For titles a library does not own, the EBL model allows each patron five minutes access to every book without a financial transaction. EBL believes that the browse period is valuable in much the way that browsing print on library shelves is valuable. EBL fairly quickly e-volved its model to include short-term loans, which are rentals paid for by a library

---

3   Personal conversation with Carolyn Morris, 2010.

on behalf of its patrons. With EBL's short-term loans the library pays a percentage of the list price of a book, depending on loan length, which can be as short as 24 hours or as long as a month, and as low as 5 percent of the list price. MARC records for all of the EBL titles a library wishes to include in a collection can be loaded into the library catalogue.

Today, librarians around the world work with EBL to build lists of titles they want to make available to their patrons. Institutions can send their holdings to EBL to avoid duplication of content. The EBL system enables libraries to make purchases either automatically after a number of short-term loans the library sets or after the library approves an alert when books are used. Additional features are detailed in Table 1. EBL has found that the short-term loan option allows libraries to control spending and to avoid surprises in which, for example, large numbers of books are purchased at once. Perhaps most important, it enables even small libraries to allow patrons access to tens of thousands more titles than the library could ever afford to buy.

Many libraries make almost the entire EBL catalogue available to their patrons. Librarians are finding it increasingly easy to predict spend levels based on the number of books visible in their catalogue. Generally, the model provides compelling value for large and small libraries. As libraries bring up a PDA program either with EBL alone or with EBL and YBP together, EBL works closely with librarians to help establish an effective profile and to choose the elaborated PDA settings that will yield best results for them.

## ebrary

**ebrary** is a technology company founded in 1999, and offers more than 273,000 ebooks, manuals, and other documents from over 500 publishers. In January 2011 ebrary was acquired by ProQuest. They launched a patron-driven model in late 2010, after two years of research, significant input from librarians, and extensive pilot testing. According to ebrary President, Kevin Sayar, "We see patron-driven as a workflow rather than a business model." [4] As such, ebrary did not rush to market with a plan but spent significant time researching how patrons use titles, iden-

---

4   Personal communication from Kevin Sayar, 2010.

tifying trends in selection, and determining the tipping point for a fair charge for value. Their pilot program ran from September 2009 to the launch of the full program in October 2010.

The model identifies several trigger mechanisms for purchase, what Sayar tagged, "10/10/copy/print." Once ten pages have been viewed (excluding front and back matter), ten minutes of real use have passed in a single user session (that is, ebrary will not count it if a student takes a break), or content has been captured by copying and pasting or by printing, a purchase of the title occurs. ebrary offers several access models for content, including unlimited use, single user, and short-term loan, all at various price points. Additional details on the model appear in Table 1.

ebrary sells worldwide to individual libraries or consortia and has integrated their patron-driven model with YBP Library Services to make it easier for libraries to deliver patron-driven acquisition through existing workflows. They draw on YBP's profiling system to determine which titles make it to a selection pool (that is, which MARC records are loaded into a library's catalogue). ebrary uses the profiling structure, but casts a wider net by gathering content that may not have made it into a traditional print approval plan. Their pilot testing showed that libraries were amazed by some of the purchased titles, which support the curriculum, but would not have been bought in a print approval plan. According to Sayar, "With data comes better decisions; we plan to analyze the data to maximize library budgets and ensure a longer life-line for the budget." ebrary also feels that PDA is a piece of any overall solution and that data being gathered now will be used to create new business models.


Publisher Models

Very few publishers offer their own patron-driven models. Most partner with at least one of the aggregators to ensure their content is exposed to as many libraries as possible while they consider options as the popularity of PDA grows. Elsevier recently launched a model based on the use of ebook purchases and Cambridge University Press (CUP) is preparing to launch one in 2011.

Elsevier's "Evidence-based Ebooks Selection" proposes access to a selection of their books on ScienceDirect for 12 months "for a minimal, up-front fee determined by a percentage of the total value of content" librarians choose. According to information on Elsevier's website, at the end of 12 months, librarians can review the use statistics for the selected ebooks and "decide which titles to purchase and keep in perpetuity, priced up to the value of the initial content investment and based upon evidence-based usage of the full range of content." [5]

Responding to customer demand, Cambridge University Press designed a patron-driven model in late 2010. As does Elsevier, CUP works with ebook aggregators, but launched their own platform to integrate their ebooks with journal content. CUP's model is available to individual libraries and consortia.

In CUP's program three accesses of a book file create a purchase. Additionally, because the CUP interface is designed around book chapters, the use of three chapters in one book also triggers a purchase. Access to the front matter, references, and sample chapters is always free.

According to Erin Igoe, Library Sales and Marketing Manager, CUP has found the process to be challenging, particularly in the area of information technology.[6] To offer the business model, their access control, billing, and royalty systems must be fully integrated. Moreover, the various systems and databases that maintain title lists must be correct for purchase, guaranteeing that every page in the title displays correctly. Another challenge CUP faces is the simultaneous release of print and electronic formats. Their goal is to release all formats at once as a way to simplify the workflow of library purchasing. In the future, CUP believes that all monographs on their platform will be available through patron-driven acquisition, leaving the possibility of opening a window to textbooks.

## Benefits and Challenges of Patron-Driven Acquisition

Patron-driven acquisition models offer benefits and challenges for librarians. In general we believe that PDA is a valuable addition to traditional acquisitions processes, that it is controllable, and that it will evolve. But before attempting a PDA workflow it is important to understand and account for the advantages it can deliver and the problems it can create.

5   "Evidence-Based Selection" SciVerse, http://www.info.sciverse.com/science direct/subscriptions/evidence-based-selection. Accessed February 4, 2011.
6   Personal communication with Erin Igoe, 2010.

## Benefits

*Guaranteed use of materials* – Each title selected through patron-driven acquisitions is guaranteed at least one use. MyiLibrary believes that 80% of the titles acquired through patron programs receive additional use. In chapter 9 of this book, on the other hand, Doug Way and Julie Garrison present evidence suggesting patron-acquired titles are not so heavily used. Studies of print use show a significant gap between titles selected by bibliographers and those used by students and faculty. For example, the University of Denver recently found that 53 percent of titles purchased during 5 years did not circulate (Levine-Clark 2010). In so far as no use amounts to a bad investment, PDA at least relieves the problem.

*Return On Investment* – Because PDA titles are used, libraries see at least some return on their investment. Data from EBL suggest that libraries achieve the greatest economic gains when they use short-term loans carefully, but libraries must balance the goals of collection build-ing with providing access in ways that suit their purposes. Patron-driven acquisition models offer considerable flexibility for librarians to establish purchase trigger points and select appropriate content.

*Just-in-time Collection* – Patron-driven acquisition provides content when the user needs it without delay or interference in the research process. One clear advantage of ebooks is that they appear instantly. Most PDA models allow multiple simultaneous use of at least some titles, preventing turnaways.

*Greater Choice of Content* – Adding MARC records to a catalogue without expending funds offers a greater selection of titles for end-users, improving the prospect that people will find what they need. In effect, without buying or building a collection libraries can have better collections than they can afford outright.

*Librarian Role Enhanced* – Once PDA is established, librarians can use their time in ways other than guessing which books patrons will use, perhaps by allowing "selectors to spend more time on harder-to-find material" (Levine-Clark 2010).

*Detailed Use Statistics* – PDA purchasing models provide significant use data on titles, subjects, number of uses, and more, data that can be used in collection decisions. A good example of useful data is browse statistics. These show which books patrons look at and for how long but do not check out. The data show that patrons often find what they need from an ebook, owing to the ability to rapidly search the entire text, at no cost to the library.

*Low-risk Investment* – Librarians can experiment with a patron-driven approach with a small initial investment. They may decide to increase or to stop based on a pilot. In other words, the overhead to begin is low enough that libraries can decide about the approach based on local experience.


## Issues and Challenges

*Librarian Buy-in* – Patron-driven acquisition models change the dynamic of collection development, empowering the user to make decisions traditionally made by librarians. This requires a philosophical shift from long-standing collection practices. The collection development librarian has a critical role in establishing the institution's PDA profile and monitoring the use and purchase of content through administrative portals. But by definition the library cedes some of its authority for how monograph dollars are spent to its public. The important thing to understand is that a PDA program should not become the entire acquisitions process for libraries. PDA coexists smoothly with traditional processes, supplementing and informing them.

*Budget/Controlling Spending* – If left unmonitored, a patron-driven acquisition model can spiral out-of-control, eating up an entire pilot budget in a short time. Close monitoring of the plan is essential for success. The controls that govern some systems are very malleable. Their effects can be observed and the settings changed to make most efficient use of a budget.

*Staff Time* – Indeed, someone in a library must own the patron-driven program. If so, the "owner" can monitor and publish useful data about what patrons choose and about how they use material. The size and make-up of the PDA offering can be carefully shaped based on data that are unavailable in a print environment. Over time, as unused books age, the library may want to replace them with newer material. Overall, however, patron-driven programs generally take much less staff time than most acquisitions processes.

*Balancing the Collection* – A strong collection will address patrons' needs across a variety of subjects and will support different curricula at different levels. But, leaving choices to patrons can unbalance resources and can introduce artificially privileged areas. As Dracine Hodges points out, "There is a realistic concern that patrons, in buying for immediate need, will change the nature of academic collections over time, generating excessive amounts of purchases in one area to the detriment of building a balanced collection" (Hodges 2010).

*Disintermediation* – Will the adoption of patron-driven acquisition lead to a future where librarians or vendors are no longer necessary? John D. Riley recently explored this future stating, "We are at the beginning of a process that can best be termed 'disintermediation.' Just as travel agents, bookstores, record stores, and video stores got 'disintermediated,' . . . libraries may be facing a similar future" (Riley 2010). One way of saying this is that if we can be disintermediated, we will be disintermediated.

Patron-driven acquisition also offers challenges beyond the library. Publishers now need to rely on aggregators to lead the technology and marketing efforts, all the while leaving the choice of what is purchased to end-users. While not a completely new concept, the process starts to change the profile of the key decision-makers within the academic market. The content is no longer necessarily more important than its presentation, its title, or its discoverability. Publishers face the challenge of estimating how many "copies" they can sell if their content is now available to a possibly much larger number of potential readers, as MARC records are loaded in library catalogues. Conversely, making a larger percentage of their publications available to more potential users creates new opportunities for publishers to expand into markets with which they would not otherwise necessarily connect.

## Opportunities

Despite the genesis of patron-driven acquisition in 1999, the model as a workable tool is relatively new. Much has happened since the early days: the model has developed to better fit the needs of librarians and publishers, especially with the advent of short-term loans; more aggregators have adopted patron-driven acquisition; publishers have begun to experiment with the model; and the literature has increased significantly as dozens of libraries conduct pilot studies and publish their findings. But many opportunities exist for growth of PDA.

First, PDA offers significant opportunities for library consortia. The modern patron-driven model has not been fully implemented within consortia. Recent contracts awarded by consortia in the United States are beginning to test that application.

Second, patron-driven acquisition could be used for print. Print-on-demand and overnight delivery of physical materials could easily be used to support a patron-driven-acquisition print program, a workflow being tested successfully, for example, at the University of Vermont (Spitzform 2011). While not instantaneous, patrons who prefer print books could select the option and might even have access to the electronic version until the print arrives.

Third, as electronic content becomes increasingly integrated with and searchable via Google or a library catalogue, the PDA models could encompass journal articles, book chapters, video and audio files, or reference works. This approach might challenge the relevance of the subscription and pay-per-view models for certain institutions, such as smaller or more specialized colleges.

Finally, just as short-term loans developed from patron-driven acquisition, other business models could arise. Pricing these alternative types of access fairly would introduce new challenges to publishers, but might become interesting alternatives for libraries. As experimentation continues, interfaces develop, and data are collected, more sophisticated and cost-effective models may proliferate within the PDA landscape.

## International Outlook

Patron-driven acquisition models are gaining popularity in North America and in the United Kingdom, where some institutions are committing more funds towards the approach and many libraries are experimenting with it. Beyond these two territories, aggregators are reaching out to libraries around the world, but how quickly the model is taking hold varies by region. For example, the concept is fully integrated with the traditional book selection process in Australia, thanks largely to EBL's work with local early adopters in launching their service. Other parts of the world, on the other hand, are in the very early stages of learning about PDA.

All of the aggregators are working with institutions worldwide, and as a result they are conscious of cultural differences that affect the transaction itself. For example, certain countries will impose a different VAT (value added tax) on electronic content. In other regions, local customer service and technical support, or online FAQs and training material in different languages will be essential. Additionally, vendors may run into difficulties in countries where libraries require all their suppliers to go through a bidding process to earn the right to provide the content for a specific period.

The model's evolution will be linked to how quickly ebooks in general are adopted. It is fair to expect that certain cultures, where the role of the librarian as a selector is very strong, will take a few years to experiment with the concept, or may not adopt it at all. The financial pressures that libraries face have spread around the world over the past few years, and librarians everywhere must justify their investment in new resources. It is, however, important to keep in mind that certain cultures will require a significant shift in their perception of ebooks, first, and, second, of a model where part of the collection can be shaped by patrons' needs. Some librarians will not easily give up what they perceive as a core value of their trade and may not accept PDA. Nevertheless, opportunities for the model to grow exist in Europe and in Asia, but growth is likely to happen more slowly than it has in Australia and is happening in North America over the next few years.

A promising territory for PDA is the Middle East. New libraries are being built, and American, Canadian, Australian, and European institutions are opening satellite campuses in the region. Patron-driven acquisition offers a unique tool for these institutions to create, in effect, a ready-made collection with little effort and at great cost savings that is closely tailored to meet users' needs (see Chapter 5 of this book). The model has proven valuable in the Middle East to date and given strong focus to implement innovative procedures. We expect the region to see rapid growth in the use of PDA.

## Conclusion

Patron-driven acquisition models have gained momentum and popularity. Libraries, publishers, and content providers alike have gained valuable experience since the concept emerged in 1999. Today, experimentation remains one key aspect of this business model and introduces a true shift of influence in the book selection process. The past few years have shown that planning, flexibility, and collaboration are three key elements to establishing successful PDA programs.

The benefits and the challenges are numerous today, but testimonies strongly suggest that the long-term benefits outweigh the short-term problems for libraries and their patrons. The concept itself introduces new opportunities beyond ebook purchasing in the traditional academic market. Recent economic pressures faced by libraries around the world have sparked interest. It will be interesting to watch the business model evolve as libraries fine-tune their profiles and as publishers investigate this new way of distributing their content.

| Feature | eBooks on EBSCO*host* | Ingram | EBL | ebrary |
|---|---|---|---|---|
| Name of model, when established | Patron Driven Acquisition, 2009. | MyiLibrary Patron Select, 2007 | Demand-driven acqui-sitions, 2003 | Patron Driven Acquisition , 2010 |
| Trigger Point for purchase | Ten pages viewed, ten minutes, copy, print or down-load. | Individually negotiated | Library decides. Most purchase a title after 3 short-term loans. Some use only short-term loans and never pur-chase; others purchase after more loans or fewer. | Based on real usage during a single-user session and includes either: 10 pages viewed, excluding TOC/index 10 minutes (some exceptions apply) copy or print |
| Free browsing allowed | Yes, for up to ten pages or ten minutes after which a pur-chase is triggered. | Yes - Unlim-ited as triggers on session not time. | Yes, for not-owned titles: 5 minutes per patron for an unlimited number of patrons. For owned titles: 10 minutes per patron before a checkout registers | Yes, for nine pages or nine minutes prior to triggering a purchase |
| Type of purchase | Single, three, or unlimited user | Single and/or multiple users | All allow multiple simultaneous users | Single user and unlimited, multi-user licenses |
| Individual library or consortia deals? | Both | Both | Both | Both |
| Interlibrary Loan allowed | Lease/ Short-term Loan | Yes | Not usually. Short-term loans have proven a | Yes, in the context of a shared consortia collection. Short |

| Feature | eBooks on EBSCO*host* | Ingram | EBL | ebrary |
|---|---|---|---|---|
| | | | better approach than ILL | Term Loans are forthcoming. |
| Integration with approval plans | Yes | Coutts | YBP in North America, Australia, New Zealand, Middle East. Blackwell in UK, Europe, Africa. DA in Australia. | Yes, in 2011 with YBP |
| Purchase single volume of multivolume set | Yes | Yes | Yes | Not possible at this time. |
| Purchase chapters only | Not at this time. | At publisher's discretion | Not possible at this time. | Not possible at this time. |
| Short-term loan options | Yes, 1, 7, 14, or 28 days. | Yes | Yes. From 24 hours through 28 days | Forthcoming, 2011. Day, week, and month planned. |
| MARC records load frequency | Default is monthly, library can change default. | Weekly | If libraries have a profile with EBL, records sent monthly. If the profile is with EBL through YBP, records come weekly. | Customers download the records, and can do so immediately after adding titles to their PDA selection. |
| Title selection provisions | Price, publisher, publication date, subject, content type (eBook or audio book) | Price, publisher, publication date, subject, bibliographic format | Price, publisher, publication date, subject | Subject, publisher, price, publication date, and other key parameters |
| Bibliographer Mediation (option to get approval for purchase) | No | Yes | Yes | No |
| Automatic Purchase | Yes | Yes | Yes, or alert library to number of uses or to price if above limit. | Yes, once triggers are reached, titles are automatically purchased. |

| Feature | eBooks on EBSCO*host* | Ingram | EBL | ebrary |
|---|---|---|---|---|
| De-duplication with existing collection | Yes | Yes | Yes | Yes, from customers' existing ebrary collection; other holdings upon request. |
| Deposit Accounts | Yes | Yes | If the library wishes. Not required. | Yes, for any amount. |
| Expenditure alerting | Yes | Yes | Yes | Yes, when funds are down to 10% or when there are not enough funds to purchase a triggered title. |
| Use reports (COUNTER, SUSHI, ICOLC?) | Yes COUNTER | Yes - COUNTER | Yes - COUNTER. By books browsed, lent, purchased, and others | Yes - COUNTER |
| Real-time delivery | Yes | Yes | Yes for owned or non-owned titles | Yes, for purchased titles |
| Fund Code Management | Yes | Yes | Yes | Yes |
| Unique Features of your PDA model | Provides a free service utilizing librarians who create customized collections tailored to libraries' unique curricular/ collection development needs. | Triggers on sessions, not time in book. Fully integrated into print approval program. | Short-term loans. Price limit alerts. Auto or manual purchasing. All titles multiple users. | Administrative functions consolidated within the ebrary interface. Create and modify automatic notifications for newly available titles of interest. |

Table 1. Comparative chart of ebook-aggregator patron-driven business models.

# References

Hodges, Dracine, Cyndi Preston, and Marsha J. Hamilton. "Patron-Initiated Collection Development: Progress of a Paradigm Shift." *Collection Management* 35 (2010): 3, 208-221.

Levine-Clark, Michael. "Developing a Multiformat Demand-Driven Acquisition Model." *Collection Management* 35 (2010): 201-207.

Norris, Brad. "NetLibrary Thanks Colorado Alliance Members." *DataLink The Alliance Newsletter* (June 1999): 4.

Riley, John. "Patron Driven Acquisitions from the Point of View of a Traditional Vendor. " *Against The Grain* 22 (2010): 5, 78-79.

Spitzform, Peter. "The User Knows Best: Patron Driven Acquisition and the Death of Expertise." Presentation at the New England Technical Services Librarians Annual Spring Conference (April 2011). College of Holy Cross. Worcester, Massachusetts.

# Chapter 9
# Financial Implications of Demand-Driven Acquisitions: A Case Study of the Value of Short-Term Loans

Doug Way and Julie Garrison
*Grand Valley State University Libraries*

Selecting ebooks as part of the overall collection-development strategy in academic libraries has become commonplace. For most, electronic collections are becoming increasingly important as libraries strive to provide greater access to material twenty-four hours a day and beyond the library walls. As budget dollars migrate toward these acquisitions, libraries are looking for ways to determine the overall effect ebooks have on their collections. Because multiple models exist for adding ebook collections and for measuring their use that are impossible with print, academic libraries have investigated costs and benefits using a variety of criteria.

The models for collecting ebooks are diverse. Libraries can add large collections at a lump cost, subscribe to dynamic collections for a fee, acquire title-by-title, purchase upon patron discovery, lease books, or choose a combination of these or other options. Many libraries are moving toward models where patrons are making selections at the point of need. To do this, the libraries add large record sets to the catalogue allowing patrons to discover and access the titles, sometimes triggering a lease or purchase. Studies validating the practice of purchasing print to fill patron interlibrary loan requests have existed for years, demonstrating that materials selected by patrons are used as heavily, if not more heavily, than those acquired by librarians (Way 2009). Few studies, however, have looked at whether patron selection continues to be valid when expanded to patron-selection of electronic books, and very little has been written to examine the costs and benefits of this practice.

In 2008 the Grand Valley State University (GVSU) Libraries began to explore implementing a PDA model for ebook collections. Compelled by earlier success in implementing PDA for interlibrary loan, an increased preference toward collecting monographs in electronic format, and the need to reallocate librarian time from collection building to other activities, the library decided to trial expanding its PDA program to ebooks.

GVSU is a comprehensive university with about 24,000 students, more than 200 undergraduate areas of study, and 27 graduate programs, almost entirely at the master's level. The University emphasizes faculty teaching over research, and graduate studies generally focus on professional programs in areas such as health care, education, and business. The library concentrates on building current collections that emphasize breadth of coverage over depth. Liaison librarians normally serve more than one major or program and are often generalists who have limited expertise in some of the areas they serve. In this environment offering a PDA option for acquiring ebooks seemed to present an attractive strategy for expanding collections.

## Literature Review

### Patron-Initiated Collecting

As early as 1999, the literature was beginning to examine the practice of patron-driven acquisitions in libraries. Perdue and Van Fleet (1999) reported that their efforts to shift from interlibrary loaning of current print monograph requests to purchasing these materials resulted in positive collection trends. Books purchased through their program circulated at a higher rate than firm orders and the program was judged to be cost effective.

This validation of print PDA has been affirmed in subsequent studies. Allen et al. (2003) piloted programs in one public and two academic libraries. They reviewed the length of time to receive items, patron satisfaction, and the average cost per book. Additionally, a review of titles added to the collection was performed at one library. In all three libraries, the programs were considered successful based on criteria outlined, including higher rates of circulation of PDA materials compared to those acquired more traditionally and patron satisfaction with the program. Purdue University, the only institution in the study to analyze titles acquired, noted that their bibliographers concluded that "a very high percentage of on-demand titles were appropriate for the collection" (30-31). More recently, Grand Valley State University Libraries (Way 2009) and University of Nebraska-Lincoln Libraries (Tyler et al. 2010) evaluated their ILL purchase programs, noting the same higher circulation for PDA materials. Way went further in his analysis, reviewing peer libraries to determine whether acquisitions made through the program were owned in other comprehensive libraries. By considering libraries with similar budgets and scope, Way found that "59% of the purchased titles were owned by at least one of the peer institutions" and that "items owned by at least one peer institution circulated more often" (305-306).

As models proffered by ebook suppliers mature, libraries are beginning to implement and evaluate PDA as a strategy for ebook acquisitions. Given the seamless nature of the ebook transaction, one concern is that PDA in an electronic environment may not yield the same sort of successful results as it has for print. Concerns over spending large sums of money developing skewed collections of little or no general interest are some of the reasons given for avoiding ebook PDA programs. Price and McDonald sought to challenge the assumption "that patron-driven selection inevitably results in purchasing of ebooks that no one (or no one else) is interested in" (2009, 2). Using EBL-hosted ebooks, Price and McDonald investigated whether user-selected (patron-acquired) or pre-selected (librarian-acquired) books were used more frequently and they analyzed the breadth of the materials collected through each strategy. They concluded that user-selected books saw heavier use and were comparable in breadth and scope to those acquired through pre-selection. The University of Denver is only beginning to consider how to evaluate their ebook acquisition program (Levine-Clark 2010). They are offering patron access to ebooks through a variety of vendors. Patrons can order books under $125 without mediation by a librarian. While no analysis has yet been done, they are planning to conduct surveys of patron preferences, gathering use data, and comparing acquisitions with materials choices selectors would have added to the collection.

## Cost/Benefit of Ebooks

While PDA is a relatively new strategy for acquiring ebooks, collecting ebooks is not new. Academic libraries have been grappling with how to measure the benefits of adding ebooks to their collections through a variety of approaches. Studies have compared use data for ebooks with circulation data for their print counterparts (Littman and Connaway 2004; Christianson and Aucoin 2005); have analyzed use of ebooks across disciplines (Bailey 2006; Christianson 2005; Christianson and

Aucoin 2005); or have surveyed faculty, staff, and student preferences (Gregory 2008; Hernon et. al 2007; Levine-Clark 2006).

Few studies, however, have analyzed the cost of acquiring ebooks. Sprague and Hunter (2009) started to address the question of whether ebooks are cost effective in collection development. As part of their analysis of ebook titles bought as collections, they calculated an approximate price per title at $1.97 and price per use at $3.67 based on information gleaned from contracts and use figures. The 130 titles "purchased individually cost, on average, $85.26 per title and $60.57 per use" (155). Individually selected and purchased titles were accessed at a higher rate than ebooks in packages, and the authors concluded that individually selected titles had been more valuable to users than titles acquired through ebook packages. They noted that owing to the differences in ebook pricing models and difficulties in comparing use data from multiple vendors, analysis is somewhat limited.

Another case study from the University of Westminster (Grigson 2009) aimed to take the evaluation of ebook models a step beyond cost-per-use metrics and sought to "compare the value for money offered by different e-book business models from two different suppliers" (62). Grigson suggests that "given the potential number of non-cost variables in a particular business model" (63) multiple ways of measuring value have to be considered. The analysis included comparing renewal options (full collection versus the ability to choose a set number of selected titles) and models for purchasing individual ebooks and limiting use. By combining a variety of metrics, Grigson was able to analyze historical use trends and identify the best vendor business-model options depending on library use patterns.

But Grigson did not consider PDA, and developing models for ebook PDA is complex. One of the unknowns libraries face entering into ebook PDA programs is how to budget appropriately and how to select the model that will yield greatest value for the institution. Libraries are experimenting with the variables vendors offer, including price ceilings for titles acquired through PDA, adjusting numbers of loans before purchase and loan periods, limiting the copyright dates of ebooks loaded, and restricting the title list available to users. All affect budgets. The University of Texas at Austin Libraries (UT) allocated $300,000 to experiment with Ebook Library (EBL), piloting a PDA program (Macicak & Schell 2009). They loaded approximately 85,000 titles into their catalogue for patrons to discover and use at the point of need. They "restricted the record load to EBL titles priced under $700, and opted to mediate any STL [short-term loan[1]] transactions priced at $50 or more" (S32). At the end of their pilot, they had spent $286,849 on the program, $190,043 on loans and $96,806 on purchases. Conclusions were that they may need to lower their price ceiling from $700 and review the $50 mediation trigger. Ohio State University Libraries (OSUL) experimented with ebrary's PDA program, initially setting up a $25,000 deposit account and implementing an 18-week test (Hodges, Preston, and Hamilton 2010). Materials were excluded from the pilot load if they were pre-2007 imprints, cost over $299.99, were from a selected list of publishers, or covered certain subjects. The deposit account was depleted within four weeks, with a total of 450 titles purchased in that time. Users triggered an average of 12 purchases per day, resulting in a daily cost of about $1,150. A second test included a broader set of titles, 43,000 ebooks, with imprint dates back to 1866. Of these, 1,242 were viewed in 37-days, the same number of days the first test was available. No cost information is provided for the second test. OSUL concluded that to implement an ebook PDA program, it could cost as much as $418,000 a year and suggested that "the amount of patron use that triggers a purchase must be set far higher than present models" (220).

At this point, libraries in North America are getting used to these models and trying a variety of ways to determine their real cost and value to the institution. The answer does not appear to be in dollars alone, but includes several variables. Up to this point, studies have focused on content quality and costs of purchasing material, but none have investigated the potential cost savings of implementing an ebook PDA program or identified models for budgetary planning, which are questions GVSU sought to answer in our evaluation.

## Project Overview

A variety of reasons led to implementing PDA at GVSU. The library knew from its own experiences and the extensive literature on PDA in areas like interlibrary loan that this was a valid and successful method

---

1    Editor's Note: In the study cited, short-term loan meant that the library rented a book on behalf of a patron and was charged a percentage of the list price, usually 5 percent to 15 percent, for the rental. When the cost of the rental was $50 or more, the library intervened to decide whether to allow the loan.

of collection development. The library hoped to adjust its collection development practices to free liaison librarians for other activities, such as closer collaboration with faculty in areas like instruction and scholarly communications. Part of our plan was to implement narrowly defined approval plans to acquire core titles that the liaisons were generally already purchasing through the library's primary book vendor. Another part of the plan was to allocate a percentage of collection funds for PDA to provide access to books in a just-in-time model. A final reason behind the move was to simply increase the universe of books immediately available to our users.

After deciding to implement PDA, GVSU decided to use EBL as the vendor for the project. The decision was based primarily on the quality of EBL's platform; the flexibility of its model; and the content, size, and scope of its catalogue. For GVSU, EBL's platform had advantages over its competitors. Like most other ebook platforms, users can print and copy and paste from books, but unlike many platforms, which place arbitrary limits on these actions, EBL uses percentages to determine how much one can print or copy and paste. Additionally, EBL's platform allows users to download books for reading off-line and for loading to ebook readers. EBL's use model at the time was also very different from other vendors' and is in some ways much more an access than a purchase model. Users can browse ebooks for a short period before a "loan" is triggered. If a user tries to download a book or copy and paste or print, they are also prompted to accept a loan. Libraries can decide what happens when a loan occurs. A library can choose to automatically purchase the book at that point or choose to lease the book, which EBL calls a Short-Term Loan (STL). The length of the loans can be from one day to twenty-eight days, and the library has the ability to set its length. The cost of one-day STLs generally ranges from 5 percent to 20 percent of the list price of the book. Libraries can mediate the purchase or loan of a book or they can have them occur automatically in a fashion that is seamless to the patron. GVSU elected to use one-day STLs and to mediate loan-requests where the cost of an STL would be more than $40.00 US.

In addition to selecting the length of STLs, the library had to choose a default access option. EBL has two main access options for its ebooks. Nonlinear Lending (NL) allows multiple users to access books, but these books have a limited number of loan-days per year, which is generally 325 days, although for some publishers it is 200 days per year. Unless the library purchases another "copy," once the loan days are exhausted, users cannot access that book for the rest of the year. The loan days available for each book reset on the anniversary of its purchase. Books available with the NL option generally cost the same as a cloth print book. EBL also sells some books with unlimited access (UA). These books generally cost more than their print equivalent, but access is not restricted to a specific number of use days. GVSU selected NL books as its default choice for auto-purchases. That meant if a book was available with both NL and UA models, the NL will be auto-purchased. The reasoning behind this primarily had to do with the lower cost of NL books and the belief that it would be rare for a book to be used so much that its use days would run out.

During the first half of 2009 GVSU worked with EBL to establish its account and to work out technical and billing issues. The library was uncertain as to how much this project would cost, as there were no case studies of PDA implementations at universities like GVSU. As a result the library guessed at what would be spent and budgeted $150,000 for the project, funded by a combination of reallocating 10 percent of current book-budget dollars ($70,000) and general-collections dollars ($80,000). GVSU established a deposit account with EBL. We requested that EBL generate an invoice for titles purchased and then attached an order record to each purchased book. This provided the library with a means to suppress all EBL records that had no order record, if that ever became necessary.

To further limit the library's risk of depleting its funds, only English-language monographs and those books published since 2005 were loaded into the catalogue. There was no de-duplication of these books other than to exclude all titles from Springer, which the library acquired directly from the publisher through a consortial agreement. As library staff come across duplicates (ebook/ebook or print/ebook) we suppress the EBL version, but based on the small number of duplicates that other libraries had found when they loaded EBL records in their catalogues it was felt that the time and energy placed in identifying duplicate titles at start-up would not be worth the cost savings it might achieve (Hardy and Davies 2007). In the end, about 50,000 titles were initially loaded into the library's catalogue.

Determining the appropriate point to purchase titles was another consideration. Given the way the EBL model works we felt that there was likely to be an optimal number of STLs and that one would not want to lease a book more than necessary before purchasing it. Lacking evidence on which to base this decision, we decided to purchase titles on the third loan. As with the budget for this project, the decision was simply an educated guess. We hoped that if a book was lent three times it would continue to see a high number of loans going forward, making the early purchase a wise alternative, saving money compared with the cost of continuing to use loans.

In addition to the books that were part of the patron-driven acquisitions project, GVSU librarians also had the option of purchasing EBL books that were not loaded into our catalogue. These EBL titles would be ordered through YBP Library Services, the library's primary book vendor. Librarians were not required to purchase EBL titles, but did so when appropriate to their normal collection-development process. Librarians were able to begin purchasing these books in fall 2009, the same time as the PDA titles were made available for use by library patrons.

In fall 2009, GVSU made approximately 50,000 EBL monographs available for use in its online catalogue. The library did nothing to promote the availability of these books other than making them discoverable in the catalogue and in Summon, the library's web-scale discovery service. Each month the library loaded about 1,000 new titles supplied by EBL that met its initial criteria, and by the end of one year about 64,000 EBL titles were available to library users.

To analyze the success of the program GVSU gathered descriptive statistics that examined the use of titles and the amount the library spent during the 12 months. The library then analyzed that data, establishing metrics like cost per use. The library also examined any savings achieved through this program and whether the library should make any changes to maximize its cost savings.

## Descriptive Statistics

### Use of Collection

The library considered use of ebooks as one factor in determining the program's success. To accomplish this, GVSU used the COUNTER BR1 report, which calculates the "successful number of title requests." Using the BR1 report to look at a 12-month period from fall 2009 through summer 2010 the library found that 6,239 unique titles were accessed a total of 10,514 times (Table 1). The average title was accessed 1.69 times, while the median and mode accesses were one.

Second, the library examined the loans for each book. A loan can be viewed as a measure of intensity of use. A user casually browsing an EBL book or accessing a book for a short time will not trigger a loan, but a user who wants to print from a book, copy and paste from a book, or who reads the book for an extended period will be prompted to accept a loan. During the 12 months examined there were 5,251 loans for 3,696 books. Of that number, 4,572 were STLs. An additional 343 loans triggered the auto-purchase of books. And finally, 336 loans occurred after books had been purchased either by librarians or through auto-purchases.

| Title Accesses | Times Accessed | Average Access / Title | Number of Loans | Number of Ebooks Loaned | Number of STLs | Number of Auto-purchases | Number of loans after Auto-purchase |
|---|---|---|---|---|---|---|---|
| 6,239 | 10,514 | 1.69 | 5,251 | 3,696 | 4,572 | 343 | 332 |

Table 1. Use of PDA titles over twelve months from fall 2009 through summer 2010.

## Cost of Access

During the 12 months examined, the library spent $68,838 on auto-purchases and STLs. The 343 books auto-purchased cost $26,947, while STLs cost $41,891. Purchased books ranged from $855 for *Modern Aspects of Rare Earths and their Complexes* to $3.99 for books like *The Great Gatsby* and *As You Like it*. In addition, librarians purchased 25 EBL books through YBP at a cost of $2,923.

The dollars spent on auto-purchases and STLs were well under the library's $150,000 budget and are far less than what it would have cost to purchase these books outright. Based on price data provided by EBL, the cost to purchase the 6,239 books accessed during the year would be $550,464. These books ranged from $3.95 for *The Communist Manifesto* to $3,000 for the *Encyclopedia of Pharmaceutical Technology*.

## Data Analysis

### Cost Per Use

Table 2 shows the cost per use for all books used in the PDA program, all EBL ebooks purchased by librarians, and all auto-purchased ebooks. The data were calculated by adding the amount spent on STLs and book purchases and then dividing the number by the number of COUNTER uses for those books. As the Table shows, librarian-selected books had the highest cost-per use because only ten of the twenty-five librarian-selected books saw any use in the first year. Auto-purchased books had a higher cost per use than the larger universe of all PDA books. Part of what drove down the cost per use for the larger universe of books was that 2,536 of the books used never triggered a loan.

| | $ Spent on Purchases | $ Spent on STLs | Total $ Spent | COUNTER Uses | Cost Per Use |
|---|---|---|---|---|---|
| All Used PDA Ebooks | 26,946.90 | 41,891.49 | 68,838.39 | 10,451 | 6.57 |
| All Librarian Purchased Ebooks | 2,923.43 | 0 | 2,923.43 | 63 | 46.40 |
| All Auto-purchased Ebooks | 26,946.90 | 6,654.40 | 33,601.30 | 2,591 | 12.97 |

Table 2. Cost per use of PDA and librarian-purchased ebooks.
Cost Per Use = (Total $ of STLs + Total $ of Purchased Books) ÷ Total Number of COUNTER Uses

### Cost Savings from PDA

Again, had they been purchased the cost of all the EBL books that saw any use would have been $550,465, compared with the $68,838 actually spent on STLs and auto-purchases. To calculate how much was saved using this PDA model, we subtracted the amount spent on STLs and auto-purchases from the cost of all books used. The amount, $481,625.96, is nearly half of the library's total monograph budget for a year and represents a huge savings.

## Loans

The library was especially interested in examining the use of loans, in part because loans indicate intensity of use, but also because most loans were either STLs or triggered auto-purchases, both of which cost the library money. EBL's administrative reports provide statistics on STLs and on the auto-purchase of a book, which indicates the trigger of an additional loan. But there was no ready way for GVSU to determine how many times a book was loaned after it had been purchased. To examine this, EBL provided us with a custom data set on loans for owned titles.

Using these data, GVSU determined that 336 loans took place during the study period after books were purchased. Of that number, 332 loans were for auto-purchased books and 4 were for librarian-selected books. Table 3 shows the majority of the auto-purchased books saw no subsequent loans after their purchase. In addition, fewer than ten percent of the auto-purchased titles were loaned more than three times after their purchase. The librarian-selected books saw far less use than the auto-purchased titles. Only three of these books were ever loaned after they were purchased, and only one of those books was loaned more than once (Table 3).

| | Zero Uses | | One Use | | Two Uses | | Three Uses | | More than Three Uses | |
|---|---|---|---|---|---|---|---|---|---|---|
| | # | % | # | % | # | % | # | % | # | % |
| Auto-purchased Ebooks | 196 | 57% | 89 | 26% | 24 | 7% | 12 | 3% | 22 | 6% |
| Librarian-Purchased Ebooks | 22 | 88% | 2 | 8% | 1 | 4% | 0 | 0% | 0 | 0% |

Table 3. Use of PDA and librarian-purchased ebooks after purchase.

Using the loan data provided by EBL we then analyzed the appropriate threshold to auto-purchase titles. As mentioned earlier, because no data were available to guide GVSU in determining the optimal purchase point, we chose the third loan to trigger an auto-purchase, hypothesizing that one would want to minimize the number of STLs used before purchasing a title in order to keep the total cost of a purchased book as close to list price as possible. The loan data (Table 3) suggest that GVSU spent more money than it could have spent. We auto-purchased books too early, given that most books did not see use after their purchase.

Table 4 shows four possible auto-purchase scenarios for the GVSU libraries. Instead of auto-purchasing on the third loan, had we auto-purchased on the fourth, only 89 titles would have been bought, and we would have saved $14,055.11. Auto-purchasing on a fifth loan would have resulted in fewer purchased books and would have saved another $5,800. Auto-purchasing on the sixth or seventh loan would have meant buying even fewer books compared with purchasing on the fifth loan. A threshold at the sixth loan would have saved the library another $789 dollars over a fifth-loan threshold, while a seventh would have saved the library an additional $1,680. In sum, moving the threshold from the third to the seventh loan would have saved the library $21,574.99.

| | # of Ebooks Purchased | Total $ of Ebooks not Purchased | Additional STL Costs | Total Savings over Existing Plan |
|---|---|---|---|---|
| Purchase on 4th Loan | 89 | 17,382.31 | 3,327.20 | 14,055.11 |
| Purchase on 5th Loan | 58 | 24,512.55 | 4,621.09 | 19,891.46 |
| Purchase on 6th Loan | 34 | 25,722.11 | 5,041.64 | 20,680.47 |
| Purchase on 7th Loan | 22 | 26,899.83 | 5,324.84 | 21,574.99 |

Table 4. Cost projections based on setting the auto-purchase point at different numbers of STLs.

## Nonlinear Loan Days

With EBL's nonlinear lending access model, each book has a limited number of days it can be used in one year. GVSU examined the number of days each purchased book was used. While we need more experience to do a thorough analysis of the NL model, during the 12 months examined, no book came close to running out of use-days. No book was used more than half of its available days, and the most popular title used 147 accesses of the 325 available over the course of eight months. This data provided GVSU with initial validation that its decision to make NL its default model was correct.

# Discussion

## Use of Collection

During the twelve-months, 6,239 books had some use, which was approximately 10 percent of GVSU's EBL collection as it existed at the end of the year. The percentage of use is comparable with the average use of our print collections. In any year about 9 percent to 10 percent of the print monographs in the library's collection circulate. This percentage also compares favorably to other similar ebook collections at GVSU. For example, about 11 percent of the library's 50,000 ebrary titles are used yearly. While this is not to say that an ebook use is equivalent to a book circulation, if the ratio persists from year to year, then it would suggest a model that could estimate ebook use. Likewise, if one could use ratios from other ebook collections as a guide then together with print use, a model for planning and budgeting could emerge.

As mentioned above, in addition to the use of basic COUNTER statistics, loans are an important measure of use. Of the 6,239 books that saw any use, only 59% (3,693) were loaned a percentage that will be important to monitor over time. If it remains consistent, the percentage can also be used in planning and budgeting for PDA.

Another important consideration is that 2,546 books were used by patrons but never loaned, which meant these uses cost the library nothing. The ability for patrons to "browse" books is an important cost-control feature. Giving libraries assurance that random clicking or an errantly selected book will not lead to a purchase or a loan encourages libraries to make more books available. At the same time, publishers must feel comfortable that their content is not being given away, which will, we hope, lead them to make more titles available for PDA programs. Looking more broadly at the 200 most used books, 26 were not purchased and of these four had no STLs. These figures indicate that the browsing safeguards protect libraries and ensure that publishers receive payment when their books are used significantly.

## Savings from PDA

GVSU found that PDA clearly can present a library with significant financial savings. The PDA model employed allowed the library to make a large number of titles available at a very low cost. That is, the libraries spent less than $70,000 to make more than $4 million in books available to users. Libraries have always had patrons help to build collections, purchasing titles based on their requests. The EBL model allowed the library to do exactly this while saving more than $480,000 over what it would have cost to purchase all of the "requested" books that saw use over the year. Moreover, unlike the historical model of responding to patron requests, where delays between the request and the receipt of a book are routine, ebooks provide instant access to the user who finds two hours, much less two days or two weeks, an unacceptable wait.

Compared to traditional interlibrary loan (ILL), the costs of PDA are significantly lower. The $6.57 average cost per use for all PDA books accessed was far below the average ILL cost, which for us is $20.00 per title. Moreover, there is no waiting for a book to be delivered from another library, no need to educate patrons on how to use the service, nor are there any forms to fill out. With PDA, users can seamlessly access materials without ever knowing that this is a service for which the library pays. While valid concerns exist about restrictions on loaning ebooks to other libraries, the lower cost and instant access of PDA books call into question the prominent role of traditional ILL as more and more books are available through this kind of model.

In many ways, important as the financial savings that can be achieved from PDA are, the time savings that can be achieved could prove more important. By making the material available to library users in this way, our librarians did not have to take time to select these books, acquisitions staff did not have to place the orders and receive the books when they arrived, cataloguing staff did not have to process the books, and circulation staff did not have to shelve them. Workflow that was required tended to take a fraction of the time traditional selection, acquisition, and processing necessitated. Absent these tasks, librarians and staff were free to spend more time collaborating with faculty, assisting patrons, or focusing on other projects.

## Librarian-Selected Versus Patron-Selected Books

Although the number of librarian-selected books was small, it provides interesting insights. More than half of the auto-purchased books were never loaned after they were purchased, yet these books still outperformed the librarian-selected titles. Only 12 percent of the librarian-selected titles were loaned after purchase. And even though only

43 percent of auto-purchased books had loans after purchase, those auto-purchased titles had already triggered three loans, or they would not have been bought.

In addition to loans, significant differences existed in the cost per use between librarian-selected titles and auto-purchased books. The cost per use for the auto-purchased titles was $33 less than the cost-per-use of librarian-selected titles. Part of what increased the cost per use for the latter was that fifteen of the twenty-five librarian-selected titles saw no COUNTER uses.

## Changes Made

The analysis of data led GVSU to refine its PDA program. First, we expanded the number of EBL books included in the program during the fall 2010 semester. To do this we added all pre-2005 monographs that met GVSU's profile, bringing the total books in the collection to more than 132,000. To buy those books would cost roughly $15 million. The library budgeted $150,000 for its 2010/2011 PDA program. The rationale was that just under $70,000 had been spent in 2009, and for 2010-2011 we doubled the number of books available. We also expect costs to increase as more books reach the auto-purchase threshold after two years of use.

The library also made some changes to its EBL settings, some of which should save money, while others may cost money. One change that is likely to result in additional costs is the removal of price limits. To control for costs GVSU originally established a maximum STL of $40.00. If the STL of a book would come to more the patron would be prompted to fill out a request form. The library received only a handful of mediated loan requests over the first year, and we allowed every request. The original thinking behind the limits was that an STL is usually 10 to 20 percent of the purchase price of a book, so a $40.00 STL would be for a book that could cost from $200 and $800. Because the library knew encyclopedias and other very expensive reference works are available for use in EBL, the limits reduced GVSU's exposure. An examination of the cost of purchased books and of what would have been the purchase price of books used but not bought showed that our fears were unfounded. Only 59 books that saw any use cost more than $400 and of those only five were purchased. As a result of this analysis, GVSU removed any price limits on STLs. Doing so eliminates the need for students or faculty to fill out an online form, which undoubtedly deterred some users. It also provides users immediate access to a resource when they want the title. The library will review the use and cost data for the coming year and based on that analysis will determine whether to re-implement price limits.

A second change that GVSU made to its EBL profile was to raise the number of loans required to trigger an auto-purchase. We hypothesized initially that by auto-purchasing books on a third loan GVSU would save money by not having to pay for unnecessary STLs. However, the majority of books had no other loans after auto-purchase, and only 10 percent of books had more than two loans after being bought. Running scenarios to determine cost savings of auto-purchasing books on the fourth, fifth, or sixth loan showed that significant savings were to be had by increasing the number of STLs before purchasing a book. While the $14,000 in savings that would have been achieved by purchasing on the fourth loan was impressive, the nearly $20,000 saved by purchasing on a fifth loan was substantial. Additional savings could have been achieved by purchasing on a sixth loan or seventh loan, but those savings of approximately $800 and $1,600 were not significant, and GVSU felt cost-saving was only one factor to be considered when deciding the auto-purchase threshold. As a result of the study GVSU elected to purchase automatically on a fifth loan.

Areas for Future Study

While PDA has been established as a viable, important component of collection development, the study of PDA using ebooks is relatively new. As a result, many areas of further research and study would benefit libraries.

At GVSU we are interested in examining the effect of adding pre-2005 ebooks to the collection. Will these books be used at the same rate as newer titles, creating a major financial impact, or will use mirror that of print monographs, where older titles in the sciences and social sciences are less likely to be used?

We also need to examine the overall budgetary effect of PDA, both initially and over time. GVSU found that the ratio of used EBL books was similar to the ratio of books circulated and also the ratio of books used in similar ebook collections. We need to determine if this ratio holds and also if it holds for other institutions. As to budgeting for

PDA, it seems to us that the cost of implementing a PDA model such as EBL's would be highest early on. During that period, when a large backfile of books is loaded into the catalogue, high-interest titles would see high use, leading to their purchase. Over time, we expect that titles likely to prove interesting will see enough loans that they will be purchased. Once we own these books, overall expenditures should drop. What will be left are long-tail books of little or occasional interest and newly added titles. Among the new titles we assume that a fairly consistent percentage will be of great interest and that others will enter the long tail. Of course, we need to examine whether this hypothesis holds true. How long will it be before the backlist titles of real interest to our patrons are bought and expenditures level off? What percentage of new titles will be loaned and purchased each year? We are eager to learn answers to these questions.

How ebooks are used is another area to be examined. If ebook use is more concentrated on individual users accessing a book many times over a short period, it could be that one-day STLs are not the most cost-effective solution. Perhaps a seven-day STL would prove more practical and would prevent a book from being borrowed day after day by one user, leading to an unnecessary purchase. The longer STL would cost the library more initially, but in the long term could save money as many books might not reach the point of triggering an auto-purchase.

Additional research on how users react to prompts may help libraries decide how best to implement mediated loans. If asking users to fill out a form is not a significant barrier, mediation may encourage libraries to make more books available and could encourage libraries hesitant about the cost of PDA to give it a try. A study of prompts would also help establish how users react when asked to initiate a loan for a book. We found many books were never loaned. Reasons could be that users determine they do not need a book during the browse period; alternatively, they might be often able to acquire the information they need in that short time without printing or copying and pasting. On the other hand, perhaps many users are confused by the prompt and never receive full access to a title they truly need.

Further study should also help understand how libraries are integrating PDA with traditional forms of collection development such as librarian-selected titles and approval plans. What are the best ways of integrating PDA into slip and approval plans? While some libraries are using slip or approval profiles to select which PDA books to add to their online catalogues, there has been little discussion of how to adjust traditional print approval plans. Until ebook vendors can provide access to all published materials a need will remain for approval plans of print materials, and even when that apparently distant day comes, some disciplines will remain resistant to the wide-scale adoption of ebooks, especially in the humanities. How libraries and vendors adjust approval plans to take into account PDA will be of increasing interest as more and more libraries begin to implement PDA, which we expect them to do. Likewise, as libraries look to implement PDA programs from multiple vendors, an examination of best practices for merging title lists and managing ongoing de-duplication and loading of MARC records will be essential.

## Conclusion

In many ways, patron-driven acquisition has seen a radical change over the past few years even as the core principles that underlay this method have essentially stayed unchanged. Patron-driven acquisition provides libraries with the ability to vastly increase access to information to their constituencies. Rather than purchase materials in anticipation of possible use, PDA allows libraries to make materials available at the point of need. What has changed is the ability of libraries to take advantage of technology to acquire and make available the materials users want in a way that is instantaneous and seamless.

While vendors and libraries are still developing and experimenting with business and use models, our study suggests that ebook PDA may offer libraries opportunities for transforming collection-development practices and achieving significant cost savings. Given the nature of how ebooks are used, access through loans instead of purchases seems a better model for providing users with more robust, rich collections within constrained budgets. Since most ebooks are only accessed once or twice, it makes sense to pay a fraction of the list price for loans at the point of need, thereby stretching limited library resources.

To fully embrace the opportunities that ebook PDA provides, libraries should consider letting go of some of the traditional collections controls. If PDA titles tend to be used at a higher rate than printed books, and the number of materials accessed through ebook catalogues tends to mirror the rate of use in traditional collections, it may be time to accept that the quality of these materials is as good, or better than those selected by librarians. Shifting book collection dollars toward

PDA and away from selector purchases seems to offer significant advantages, especially in libraries where the focus is on developing collections that meet the current needs of their user populations. For these libraries, while PDA may never completely replace traditional forms of collection development, the continued growth of ebook catalogues and the emergence of print-on-demand technology suggest that PDA may soon become the predominant form of collection development.

# References

Allen, Megan, Suzanne M. Ward, Tanner Wray, and Karl E Debus-Lopez. "Patron-focused Services in Three US libraries: Collaborative Interlibrary Loan, Collection Development and Acquisitions." *Interlending & Document Supply* 31, no.2 (January 1, 2003): 138-141.

Bailey, Timothy P. "Electronic Book Usage at a Master's Level I University: A Longitudinal Study." *The Journal of Academic Librarianship* 32, no. 1 (2006): 52-59.

Christianson, Marilyn. "Patterns of Use of Electronic Books." *Library Collections, Acquisitions, and Technical Services* 29, no. 4 (2005): 351-363.

Christianson, Marilyn and Marsha Aucoin. "Electronic or Print Books: Which are Used?" *Library Collections, Acquisitions, and Technical Services* 29, no.1 (2005): 71-81.

Gregory, Cynthia L. "But I Want a Real Book: An Investigation of Undergraduates' Usage and Attitudes toward Electronic Books." *Reference & User Services Quarterly* 47, no. 3 (2008): 266-273.

Grigson, Anna. "Evaluating Business Models for E-Books Through Usage Data Analysis: A Case Study from the University of Westminster." *Journal of Electronic Resources Librarianship* 21 (2009): 62-74. doi: 10.1080/19411260902858623.

Hardy, Gary and Tony Davies. "Letting the patrons choose - using EBL as a method for unmediated acquisition of ebook materials." Paper presented at Information Online 2007, Sydney, Australia, January 30-February 1, 2007. http://conferences.alia.org.au/online2007/Presentations/31Jan.B8.letting.the.users.choose.pdf.

Hernon, Peter, Rosita Hopper, Michael R. Leach, Laura L. Saunders, and Jane Zhang. "E-book Use by Students: Undergraduates in Economics, Literature, and Nursing. *The Journal of Academic Librarianship* 33, no. 1 (2007): 3-13.

Hodges, Dracine, Cyndi Preston, and Marsha J. Hamilton. "Patron-Initiated Collection Development: Progress of a Paradigm Shift." *Collection Management* 35 (2010): 208-221. doi: 10.1080/01462679.2010.486968.

Levine-Clark, Michael. "Electronic Book Usage: A Survey at the University of Denver." *portal: Libraries and the Academy* 6, no. 3 (2006): 285-299. doi: 10.1353/pla.2006. 0041.

Levine-Clark, Michael. "Developing a Multiformat Demand-Driven Acquisition Model." *Collection Management* 35 (2010): 201-207. doi: 10.1080/ 01462679.2010.486965.

Littman, Justin and Lynn Silipigni Connaway. "A Circulation Analysis of Print Books and E-Books in an Academic Research Library." *Library Resources and Technical Services* 48, no. 4 (2004): 256-262.

Macicak, Susan, and Lindsay E. Schell. "Patron-Driven, Librarian-Approved: A Pay-Per-View Model for E-Books." *Serials* 22, no. 3 (2009): S31-S38.

Perdue, Jennifer and James A. Van Fleet. "Borrow or Buy? Cost-Effective Delivery of Monographs." *Journal of Interlibrary Loan, Document Delivery, & Information Supply* 9, no. 4 (1999): 19-28.

Price, Jason and John McDonald. "Beguiled by Bananas: A Retrospective Study of the Usage & Breadth of Patron vs. Librarian Acquired Ebook Collections." Claremont Colleges Library, Claremont University Consortium, 2009. http://ccdl.libraries.claremont. edu/u?/lea,175.

Sprague, Nancy and Ben Hunter. "Assessing E-Books: Taking a Closer Look at E-Book Statistics." *Library Collections, Acquisitions & Technical Services* 32 (2009): 150-157.

Tyler, David C. and Yang Xu, Joyce C. Melvin, Marylou Epp, and Anita M. Kreps. "Just How Right are the Customers? An Analysis of the Relative Performance of Patron-Initiated Interlibrary Loan Monograph Purchases." *Collection Management* 35 (2010): 162-179. doi: 10.1080/01462679. 2010.487030.

Way, Doug. "The Assessment of Patron-Initiated Collection Development via Interlibrary Loan at a Comprehensive University. " *Journal of Interlibrary Loan, Document Delivery & Electronic Reserve.* 19 (2009): 299-308. doi: 10.1080/10723030903278374.

# Chapter 10
# Texas Demand-Driven Acquisitions:
# Controlling Costs in a Large-Scale PDA Program

## Dennis Dillon
*University of Texas, Austin*

Once upon a time, like every other library, Texas bought print books and journals based on speculation, hope, and informed good intentions. While these print purchases originally seemed a wise idea, unfortunately they just were not delivering the results we wanted.

## Demand-Driven Acquisitions: Origins at the University of Texas, Austin

The impetus for demand-driven acquisitions at the University of Texas, Austin, grew out of significant purchases of ebooks in 1999. These ebooks were in all subjects from more than a hundred publishers and had widely varying publication dates. Use of the ebooks was surprisingly strong, exceeding the use of similar print books almost fifty to one. Because this high rate of use was so surprising, we analyzed the data to determine if any patterns shed light on which types of books we could expect to do well in the future.

Unfortunately, the use patterns refused to fit our preconceived beliefs, or more ominously, to match with our existing collection strategies. As a result, we continued to purchase widely in all subjects, from all publishers, in all date ranges, and to collect use data, which we would compare to the use of print in the library. One thing that stuck out in this welter was that surprisingly many books were never used. They were not used in print, they were not used electronically, they were not used in year one, or year two, or even in year ten. We librarians were buying books that no one cared about. We were wasting significant money on books while at the same time we were cancelling serials and databases that were heavily used and needed for both research and classrooms. There had to be a better way. Somehow we needed to find a way to engage the users in more of the library's purchasing decisions and to reduce the purchase of books that were never used.

We began to understand that maybe we did not know our users as well as we thought. In the course of analyzing, we soon looked into how much it cost to park a book on the shelf. We discovered that calculations on new library construction put the cost of a parking space for a book – never mind the cost of the book itself – at over $100. (The Council on Library and Information Resources later calculated the total cost of space for a book at $142.[1]) Once you started adding up the different costs – $100 to buy a book, $20 to catalogue it, and $142 to park it – you had to feel uneasy about so much money going for titles that no one used. We began to understand that the costs of buying, acquiring, and shelving each book had to be judged in an especially harsh light because 30 percent, 40 percent, or even 50 percent were never being touched by any patron. It was these revelations that led us to investigate demand-driven purchasing.

## Patron-Driven Acquisitions Begins

Our first move was to budget funds to buy books requested through inter-library loan. This worked well, and the budgeting was predictable. If we restricted purchases to books published in the past two years that cost less than $150, we found that an annual allocation of $20,000 was consistently sufficient to cover requests. User demand varied little from year to year, corresponding to library statistics in which circulation, library visits, and database use, among others, were predictable and only slightly variable. Buying books requested through inter-library loan ensured that every book was used at least once, and that the expenditures were a relatively efficient use of collection funds.

## Issues with Demand-Driven Strategies

In short, the beginning of our consideration of demand-driven acquisitions was the gradual recognition that traditional acquisitions techniques and

---

1   *The Idea of Order: Transforming Research Collections for 21$^{st}$ Century Scholarship*. Council on Library and Information Resources, Washington, D. C. 2010: 92.

collection strategies were not working as we wanted. Simultaneously, the price of big-deal e-journal packages had continued to increase. New databases, journals, and books were being produced every day, both for subscription and for outright purchase, and we did not have nearly enough money to acquire all of the resources the library needed. Existing business models did not allow libraries the flexibility to manage their collections effectively over the long term, or even to meet users' short-term needs. The only option for libraries was to spend money upfront for either subscriptions or outright purchases, and to hope that the speculative buying matched users' needs. Compounding the problem, in an effort to achieve economies of scale, many products were packaged or bundled, increasingly limiting the ability of libraries to manage our funds or to design collections to particular ends.

One pricing approach, however, offered potential to ameliorate, if not solve, these problems. This was the pricing model that had traditionally fallen under the catchall heading of use-based pricing, patron-driven acquisitions, or demand-driven acquisitions. Variations on this model had been around from the earliest days of networking, such as OCLC's block-pricing model for databases in which libraries would buy a number of block searches for a particular database upfront, and as people used the database, their searches would be deducted from the library's block allotment. The problem with such use-based pricing was that it was difficult to budget for, particularly in the early days of online databases when neither libraries nor vendors understood the potential patterns for any database or user group.

NetLibrary's customers discovered the problem in 1999 with a patron-driven ebook model that had sensitive trigger points, in which one or two uses created a purchase. Another copy was automatically purchased if the first copy was in use when a second patron tried to access the title. The result was uncontrolled spiraling expenditure. When, for example, a professor assigned a book for a test, students would leave class and access the book simultaneously. The result was that libraries could end up automatically purchasing a dozen or more copies of a title that, after the first hour's rush, was never used again by anyone. There had to be a better way.

Since ebooks are always only a click away, they can incur lots of casual use more akin to browsing than to reading. Because of this it is important that the browses *not* trigger a purchase when a reader idly scans five or six pages or browses a book for 3 or 4 minutes. Arriving at a business model that does not quickly deplete library budgets, yet provides enough revenue for publishers to willingly offer their content and that compensates them for potential lost sales was a challenge. These difficulties with patron-driven acquisitions models, particularly with budgeting, predicting use, and separating serious use from browsing, caused the approach to fall out of favor, and eventually led to both libraries and vendors preferring simpler ebook models based on subscriptions and outright purchase. True demand-driven acquisitions, by contrast, would allow demand to drive expenditures, and it would not force unwanted purchases.

The trigger points for demand-driven expenditures are in themselves a measure of the use of an item. A trigger could be the number of minutes a user reads a resource, or page views, pages printed, times accessed, or other measures, until eventually a purchase point is reached. With demand-driven programs the library can decide (within boundaries) what demands and trigger points it is willing to fund, and what titles it chooses to expose to user selection. A library may choose short-term rentals for every access of every book, for example, and set up its parameters so that no book is ever purchased. Demand-driven approaches allow a library flexibility in both pricing models and in expenditure choices.

## Learning from Experience

At the University of Texas we learned several things from our early decision to purchase books requested through inter-library loan, as we did from subsidizing article document delivery, and from purchasing large numbers of ebooks covering every subject from every publisher. We discovered over time that while ebook use was high, it was predictable. Some books were never used and others received use month after month, year after year. We needed a way to reliably predict both the expected use of a particular title and to easily manage the ebook collection with a minimum investment of staff time. Eventually we discovered, at least on our campus and on the campuses of our consortia partners, that a book's publisher was a good predictor of use. For example, books from Cambridge University Press are almost always a good investment for our user group, while books from some other publishers are almost always a bad investment. Not every Cambridge title was a winner, but overall, their books receive very high use, year after year. Further, in comparing ebook use by publisher to print book use by publisher, we discovered that high-use publishers were high-use in either format, and that low-use publishers in one format were low-to-medium use in the other. One result is that, as of this writing, we are continuing to purchase Cambridge (and a handful of other publishers) in both print and in ebook editions.

While we are confident of the publisher-based use data we have for the subjects that are researched and taught at the University of Texas and comfortable with the use we can expect from our mix of 20,000 faculty and staff and 50,000 students, we believe that use details will differ for every campus and every user group. The use rates in other settings will differ according to how many ebooks and other online content are available, and what subjects interest that community. However, once a library reaches a critical mass of ebooks and the range of titles grows large enough, the overall average use rates for individual titles drops, since users no longer need to settle for reading ebooks that are not exactly what they want. We call this the "remote access effect." When it is 3:00 a.m. or the library is 15 miles away, users are more willing to read and browse any book that is more-or-less relevant, but as the number of ebooks increases, users become more selective and restrict their reading to books that are specific to their needs.

## Implementation

Once we made a decision to give demand-driven acquisitions a try, we decided that a small trial would not return actionable information. What we needed was a broad range of subjects and a broad range of publishers that might engage a broad swath of the campus. Knowing how one user group responded to demand-driven ebooks would tell us nothing about how a different user group might respond. As a consequence we decided to begin the first year with access to from 60,000 to 100,000 titles, and to keep subsequent years in that range.

We termed this group of titles our "risk pool" and realized that while potentially we could end up buying 100,000 titles in a few months, realistically, given our rate of ebook use for new titles from these types of publishers, we could expect that probably only 2,000 titles would receive four or more serious uses during the twelve months, and that probably only 10,000 to 15,000 titles would receive serious sustained use (viewed between one and three times for more than five minutes). We also hypothesized that the vast majority (around 60 percent of the titles) would be browsed cursorily, with the user opening the link and looking at only a few pages for under five minutes. Because the vendor we chose, Ebook Library (EBL), did not charge for the first five minutes of browsing a book, we were confident that any costs we incurred would be cases where a library user was intentionally reading the content.

In the EBL demand-driven model, the reader has five minutes of free browsing before a monetized transaction happens; the library has the ability to decide what to do when the five-minutes have passed. Texas elected to pay for a 24-hour short-term rental and to automatically purchase the book on a third checkout. For us this has proven to be more productive than traditional speculative purchasing of printed books, in that it ensures every dollar is spent for books that are actually being used.

## Setting up the profile

With demand-driven programs it is always valuable to simulate the purchase trigger points based on local use data. The questions to ask are which publishers, publication dates, and subjects do your users best respond to and how often are they likely to squeeze the purchase trigger? With this information it is possible to create a profile and to budget appropriately.

We restrict our initial profiling to specific publishers and price limits as follows.

1. We keep demand-driven titles to a list price under $250, believing that higher-priced books are usually for a niche audience and typically will not be extensively used. We prefer to have library subject specialists choose such expensive titles.
2. We also buy outright the books of the very best performing publishers through print approval plans, but we also make these middle-to-top tier publishers available for demand-driven selection. In other words, we allow a demand-driven ebook to duplicate print.
3. We are now selecting a second tier of publishers to test under a different business model in case we have inadvertently jumped to conclusions and somehow skewed the data that we have been working with. Testing different publishers by adding their content to the risk pool of demand-driven content, and then evaluating the use

of their books, keeps the library honest and makes sure that that we are not becoming trapped by pre-conceived conclusions.

4. We expect bibliographers to selectively order the bottom-tier publishers.

## Budgeting

Budgeting for our demand-driven acquisitions has been so predictable that it is boring. Over the past four years expenditures have almost always been within 1 to 2 percent of our predicted budget, though the past two years the expenditures have come in under budget. We suspect that the under expenditure is because we now have so many ebooks (several hundred thousand) that our customers often find what they need without initiating a demand-driven expenditure. The key to budgeting is to know how your customers behave and not just to speculate. The first year we employed our demand-driven program it took only minutes to calculate what a risk pool of a hundred thousand patron-driven ebooks would cost over 12 months. It turned out that we had overestimated our cost by 1 percent, so in the end we were slightly under budget. In subsequent years we have miscalculated by as much as 3 percent. Since, however, we always have funds set aside for end-of-year collection emergencies we have never had reason to worry. More important, we have not been forced to use the emergency fund because we make adjustments during the year. The key to budgeting is to be data driven, to know your users, and to understand that ebooks are used at a higher rate than print, though once the library has a critical mass of ebooks, use levels off.

To budget for PDA we first determine the size of our risk pool for the year. We tend to start each year with a risk pool of 60,000 to 70,000 titles, planning to add 30,000 to 40,000 new titles over the year as they appear. At the end of each year we remove any titles that have received no use over the past twelve to twenty-four months and review both publishers and price limits to determine if we need to alter our profile. We also look at the pattern of expenditures for the previous twelve months and determine if any adjustments will be necessary. We keep track of the rate of automatic purchases (which tend to increase a bit each year as many titles in the risk pool build up a record of use) and our rate of short-term rentals (which tend to decrease each year as the library builds a critical mass of quality high-use purchased ebooks). Budgeting is not significantly different from that for a traditional print approval plan. (You could argue, in fact, that a demand-driven plan is nothing more than a traditional approval plan in which the library pays only for books that are used.) The key is to control the number and make-up of titles that comprise the risk pool, and then to determine the probable rate of use for publishers and titles based on historic data at your institution.

The most basic formula for budget calculation is [A] * [B] where [A] is the expected number of trigger events and [B] is the average cost of a trigger event. The number of expected trigger events depends on the size of the risk pool, so in calculating [A], it is wise to plan your budget based on the size of the risk pool at the end of a 12-month budget period. To arrive at [A] you decide what percent or number of titles from the risk pool will attract trigger events.

A more complex demand-driven formula and one that is akin to that used at Texas is as follows:

1. Compile the number of titles publisher by publisher to be included in the risk pool.
2. Calculate the number of expected trigger events for each publisher in the risk pool based on historic ebook use rates for each publisher by the library's user group; that is, how many titles can be expected to be used once, how many will be used twice, and so forth.
3. Multiply the trigger events for each publisher by the average calculated cost of a trigger event for that publisher. The cost of a trigger event may be the average purchase price of a publisher's books, the average short-term rental costs of their books, a percent of the purchase price of the books, or other factors, depending on the business model in use.
4. Add the potential cost for each publisher and then total the costs for all of the publishers.
5. Compare the costs, assumptions, and trends from the previous year. Adjust for changes in the size of the risk pool or the publisher mix. Again, the more ebooks your library offers, whether previously purchased ebooks, subscription packages, or whatever, the lower the rate of use of your demand-driven acquisitions because your users have a larger universe of ebooks from which to choose. Of course, the opposite is also true; fewer ebooks means the risk-pool title is likely to be used more. Use rates for individual titles at Texas dropped significantly once the OPAC had records for more than 100,000 ebooks.

6. Finally, set aside an end-of-year emergency fund in case you have miscalculated and need more money to finish the program. Texas prefers to run our acquisitions programs for a complete year in order to gather reliable data. In an academic setting use varies greatly from month to month during the academic calendar. Weeks when the library has a high use rate for humanities texts do not always correspond to the weeks of high use for scientific or engineering titles. Having 12 months of data by publisher and by call number is tremendously helpful for planning.

If you have no more than a vague idea of how patrons use your collection, then consider subscribing to a large ebook collection and gathering data before embarking on a demand-driven program.

In summary, determine the size and composition of your risk pool, calculate the expected rate of use for that number of titles from the publishers or subjects you will include, and then calculate the average costs as you reach each trigger point. If the costs appear too high, consider a vendor with a different set of trigger points or shrink your risk pool. Finally, add the costs, and you will arrive at your projected expenditure. Demand-driven programs need to be based on realistic, data-driven assessment of how your users will behave. Basing a program on assumptions or speculation can have problematic budget consequences.

## Monitoring

The first rule of demand-driven acquisitions is: Control the costs. If you continually add new content to your risk pool, costs will inevitably rise. It is critical to assign the responsibility for monitoring a demand-driven program. One person must closely watch invoices, additions to the risk pool, and shifts in use patterns. One person must own the program, must be able to report to the library what is happening at any moment and what is predicted to happen over the next months. If the program is set up properly and appropriately monitored, no invoice should be a surprise, no use pattern should be unexpected.

At Texas we have reported every demand-driven title we have ever purchased to all interested staff in an email every two weeks. The email lists the titles, publishers, dates purchased, prices; all other print or ebook copies of the titles that we own; and whether those other copies were checked out, on the shelf, on reserve, or otherwise unavailable.

The report creates a useful feedback loop and helps keep selectors informed as to what titles interest our users. We also total every invoice, add it to the year-to-date expenditures, and project expected year-end costs. We compare every month's invoice to the same month for every previous year. We collect statistics by publisher, call number, and publication dates. We note changes in use trends, being especially alert for unusual blips in use or cost. If necessary, we adjust the risk pool by adding or eliminating publishers, raising or lowering the price limits of books we allow into the risk pool, or by adjusting the trigger points that allow an unmediated short-term loan or purchase. While this may sound daunting, it takes very little staff time. It is routinized taking of the pulse of the program to make sure that no dangerous symptoms develop unnoticed.

## Lessons learned

The main lesson we have learned is that demand-driven acquisitions need to be part of the larger collection framework, integral to a system of strategies for how the library delivers content to users. In the context of the overall collection development strategy, demand-driven acquisitions has an important role for us. It is not an outlier, not isolated from the rest of the collecting effort. Because administering a PDA program is so painless, the library must be vigilant to control budgets and to prevent mission creep from enlarging the original scope. PDA operates so efficiently that libraries have to be careful not to be lulled into letting it take over ever more of the budget.

Why is PDA important? It can save hundreds of thousands of dollars each year needlessly investing in books that are not used. The library does not have to pay $142 per item to park a book on seldom visited shelves. The library does not have to catalogue the books in a PDA program but can arrange to receive cataloguing from the vendor or from OCLC. And, librarians do not have to select, order, and process individual titles. The investment of staff time in the Texas demand-driven ebook effort is too small to measure, and mostly consists of monitoring use, paying the monthly invoice, and processing the weekly bulk load of new MARC records.

Library users appreciate the quick and regular appearance of a wide selection of new titles. They are pleased at the ability to access ebooks 24/7. In cases where we duplicate a publisher in print approval plans and as a demand-driven ebook, it is now common for the ebook to be available a month before the print edition arrives. After four years, one of our few concerns is that the program runs so smoothly that it has permanently spoiled us and left us wishing our other acquisition efforts were as predictable and as trouble free.

# Reference

*The Idea of Order: Transforming Research Collections for 21<sup>st</sup> Century Scholarship.* Council on Library and Information Resources, Washington, D. C. 2010. p. 92.

# Chapter 11
## Elements of a Demand-Driven Model

David Swords
*Ebook Library*

This chapter has three purposes. First, it takes up the important differences between acquisitions thinking as we have practiced it for decades, and thinking in a demand-driven, ebook environment. Second, it describes the elements that make a demand-driven acquisitions workflow practical. And third, it presents a model for budgeting for PDA. These three issues – how is PDA thinking different from past thinking, what does a PDA system require to be workable, and how do you budget for it – are essential to establishing a viable PDA program. Many libraries are still experimenting with PDA, dipping a toe gingerly into its strange waters. And that's fine. But the workflow at this point really is not experimental. Implementing, operating, and overseeing PDA as a significant, valuable part of a library's process for presenting monographs to its patrons can be done confidently on a larger scale than many libraries realize and with important benefit.

## "We don't know who discovered the water, but we know it wasn't the fish." (*Marshall McLuhan*)

Use-driven acquisition is sometimes described and evaluated as a tool for saving money and sometimes regarded skeptically as a way of spending far too much. Neither description, however, is accurate. The tales about tens of thousands of dollars being gobbled up in days or weeks (see, for example, Hodges, Preston, and Hamilton 2010) came mostly from early experiments with models that were unsophisticated or unfinished. And while the notion that PDA can save money is true in an accounting sense, rather than use it to reduce spending, using PDA to make a library better – useful more of the time to more people – is a wiser way to deploy it.

Every library has limits to the number of books it can buy and in the past has taken its best guess about what patrons need in the present or might need someday. The extent of the guess is based on the size of the budget. Small libraries with small budgets can buy only a tiny fraction of the monographs that appear in a year, and a diminishingly smaller percentage of the universe of books that are available. But even institutions with enormous budgets cannot buy close to everything. In this, PDA can help.

The power of PDA is that it extends the number of books a library can make accessible to patrons. For the same money that a library would spend if it bought books outright, many libraries make available 25, 50, 100, or more times the number of solid academic titles accessible to patrons by means of a PDA program. It is almost tautological to say that if, without increasing its budget, a library can make more books accessible it becomes a better resource for its patrons and an easier budget defense for its administrators.

Table 1 cites three representative examples.[1] Each library makes more than 100,000 ebooks accessible through its PDA program. The cost of providing the books appears in the "PDA Expenditures" column; the data are for December 2009 through December 2010. The figures in the far right column are derived by multiplying the average price each particular library spent on books it purchased during the year times the number of visible titles. The Australian library supports a science curriculum and the average price of books it bought was about $95 (all amounts are USD). The other libraries support broad curricula; the average cost of books they bought was closer to $75.

| Institution | PDA Titles | PDA Expenditure (USD) | Number of Patrons | Cost to Buy All Visible Titles (USD) |
|---|---|---|---|---|
| Australian University, Victoria | 121,423 | $201,255 | 22,046 | $11,581,326 |
| US University, New Jersey | 151,237 | $40,048 | 15,051 | $11,243,000 |
| US University, California | 143,883 | $31,031 | 3,414 | $11,137,000 |

Table 1. Visible titles with actual expenditures compared to estimated cost to purchase the same titles. Based on PDA programs at libraries serving different numbers of patrons. Data are for one year, December 2009 to December 2010.

If each library had spent its budget buying books from among those it made accessible, the number of books it could have purchased would

---

1    All data in this chapter are from Ebook Library (EBL).

have been, from the top of the Table to the bottom, 2,108; 539; and 401. Said differently, the Australian university was able to allow access to 67 times the books it could have bought for $201,000; the New Jersey library made 281 times more books available than it could have bought for $40,000; and the California library, made 359 times the number of books accessible compared with what it could have bought for its $30,000 budget.

The numbers are striking evidence that a PDA program can make it possible for library users to find what they need more of the time than would be likely in a purchase program. In general, it will cost more to make lots of titles accessible at large institutions than at smaller ones; the ratio of visible titles to expenditures declines as the the size of the institution increases. On the other hand, as data later in the chapter demonstrate, the ratio remains high. A well administered PDA program, even at a research library such as the University of Texas at Austin, can still make 15 to 20 times more titles accessible than the library could buy for the same budget. The column that shows Number of Patrons is important, but not decisive, in modeling a PDA program, and its effect will be described more fully later.

If the numbers of books to which a library can allow access in a PDA program is perhaps surprisingly large, the number is also quite terrifying. When your budget is $25,000 and you are about to give your patrons nearly unfettered access to more than 100,000 expensive academic books, after decades of ever so carefully choosing among the few hundred you could afford to buy, who would not be cautious? And with tales of budgets busted in a month afoot, how could one not be skeptical?

A typical approach to PDA plays out as follows. A library that serves 12,000 to 15,000 students allocates $25,000 to a PDA experiment that it expects to last from six months to one year. The library selects a handful of subject areas. Immediately, questions about which books to include and which to omit arise.

The essence of PDA – you pay only for what gets used seriously[2] – should fundamentally change approaches to acquisitions. Yet, as libraries try PDA programs, their approach tends not to change. When the job is to think about what to include rather than what to buy, constraints imposed by the possibility that a book will be an expensive failure disappear. But the thinking that applies in longstanding acquisitions

---

2    "Seriously," a vague term, stands in here for the specific criteria different aggregators apply before a library pays for use.

practices almost inevitably imposes itself on PDA, at least in the beginning.

Here are some examples of how academic libraries generally approach buying monographs:

1.  Most of the time they buy books as they are published, when they first appear. Certain tools, such as approval plans, are all about new books.
2.  Libraries avoid duplication whenever they can.
3.  For reasons that are philosophical, psychological, and cultural, as much as they are economic, libraries mostly exclude low-level books such as guidebooks and self-help material.
4.  Nearly every approval plan has price caps that turn automatic books to slips. A common threshold is $150 because a shelf-bound book at that price is equivalent to two $75 books, three $50 books, or six $25 books.

Consider now the library that wants to implement a PDA experiment with a budget of $25,000. Let us say the test will involve three subjects, psychology, business, and education. Again, the library serves roughly 15,000 students and faculty, but the subset of patrons interested in the subjects covered will be much smaller, probably no more than 3,000, at the very outside 5,000.

What often happens with PDA is that the library, guided by long-standing best practices, will limit the books it includes to (1) those published in the past two years, (2) titles that do not duplicate other holdings, (3) things that are not low level, and (4) books that cost less than $150. Other exclusions could be certain publishers, perhaps because their titles traditionally are very expensive or not as sound as the library likes. The result is that, depending on the subjects, as few as 2,500 but no more than 5,500, books make the program. In a recent example a library that fits the profile used here took this approach and spent slightly more than $1,000 during the first three months of its PDA program. The library began with 5,500 books but could have safely included 30,000 to 40,000 in the program. The simplest way to have included lots more books would have been to step away from those precepts. Here is what I mean.

Why not include "old" books in a PDA program? It costs nothing to add them, and only if someone makes use of a book published in 2000 or 2005 will a charge occur. In the past we have bought new books partly because various tools such as notices from publishers and approval plans put them before us when they were new. But least is known about books when they are new, and with the exceptions of certain genres such as computer manuals, publishers expect books to remain relevant for longer than a couple of years. Another way to think about it is what is the mean age of the print books on your library's shelves today? Thus, giving patrons access to titles a few years old, that will cost you nothing until they are used, really is not a huge step.

Why duplicate? You would NOT duplicate titles in a PDA program to which you already have electronic access. But if you own the print consider adding the ebook. It costs nothing. Patrons could prefer the electronic version, and you obtain useful data about their preferences. They can check out the ebook from the dorm at 3:00 in the morning that their paper is due and do not ever have to carry it back to the library later. If during the hours the library is open they find the print is checked out, they need not await its return.

Why include low-level books? Well, it costs nothing. You can counter that "dummies" titles or popular treatments are the ones students will use, so they will have costs, and by including them we move students away from more authoritative books, the kind they should be using. I cannot, would not argue the point, which goes to the fundamental identity of a library. Most academic libraries will leave them out. But one reason to consider low-level books is that if they are included, they will be used. This has been true whenever libraries include them.

Why include expensive books? They are expensive because they have something to contribute in some specialized field. In a PDA environment, if an expensive book goes unused, the library suffers no consequence, pays nothing. If it turns out to be used beyond an access period, the library need not pay full price, setting the first few uses to be short-term loans. When you must buy a book to make it accessible, $150 is a big risk. In a PDA workflow, you pay nothing to make the book accessible. You might spend $10 or $15 for loans. If the book were borrowed many times, then spending $150 on it is a good investment.

The real point here is not to persuade you to dismiss old practices summarily. Rather it is to suggest that they will be there tugging at your decisions. In the 1980s as libraries moved from card catalogues to online systems, the ILS's duplicated the functionality of index cards in the online catalogue, oversimplifying what could have been a much more robust means for searching. As you undertake a PDA program the considerable consequences of not having to buy books to make them available deserve to be considered in their own right, outside the constraints that guide our current acquisitions practices. PDA programs are by their nature inclusive where other acquisition methods have tended to be exclusive. Old considerations about price, buying before a book has a history, and duplication either disappear or are greatly ameliorated. But the shift from print to ebooks, and especially from buying new books upon publication to use-based acquisition, requires the equivalent of a culture shift. The difference in thinking between providing access and building a collection is considerable. The acquisitions practices we have used for so long are themselves the results of technology and not laws of nature.

## The Elements of a Successful PDA Model

PDA is in its infancy and the ways in which it is practiced will change, but certain characteristics seem likely to endure into the unpredictable future just as others have already proven to be unsuitable. We know that where systems count clicks leading up to a purchase libraries end up buying too many books and books in which people have no real interest. By contrast, a browse period that allows limited time but unlimited access during that time and that gives every patron their own chance to investigate each book works very well. In this section we will describe what have emerged as the most important characteristics of a PDA program.

It is elemental but worth noting that books in a PDA program have a more complex identity than the books that live on a library's shelf. Traditionally, a library buys a book and the book is available to patrons, end of story. In a PDA program, the library specifically does not buy most of the books, which exist as MARC records in its catalogue. They are there, but you do not own them and pay nothing for their presence. Next, someone searches the catalogue, finds one of these books, links out and looks to see if it is what they need. We can call this an examination or browse period, but during this limited time, the library does not pay for the patron to have access. Next, if the patron needs the book, wants a loan, the library may rent it on their behalf. In this condition, now being called a short-term loan (STL), the library pays a percentage of the list price of the book for the patron to have access; the longer the loan, the greater the cost, though it is still far less than buying the book. Finally, after a book has been lent a certain number of times, the library usually will purchase it automatically. The result of this chain of events is that a library pays nothing for most of the books in the program, because they are never used at all or never used beyond an examination period. The library pays something far below the purchase price for another large subset of lightly used books. And finally, the relatively few books that are used a great deal, the library typically buys. Understanding these conditions is necessary background to understanding the capabilities required for a PDA model to work effectively.

## Examination Period

Limited but adequate access to titles that enables each patron to determine whether any book is likely to serve their needs at no cost to the library is key. One way this piece of a PDA model can be implemented is to allow a finite examination or browse period during which a patron can look through books the library does not own. At the end of the period the patron either requests a loan, for which the library pays, or sends the book back to its virtual shelf, in which case no charge occurs. During the browse period patrons may learn that a book lacks what they need, has what they need and can be mined before a loan occurs, or that they require a loan.

In early PDA models, "touches" rather than a browse period decided the fate of a book. For example, in some models the second time a patron opened a book the library bought it. A browse period, by contrast, means that a book can be found by dozens or hundreds of people in the course of their research. Its metadata can be reviewed. It can be searched for every occurrence of a word, and the investigator can jump to each to understand the context. Only at the end of the browse period (usually five or ten minutes) or if the patron decides to copy, print, or download, does a transaction eventuate.

Browses have value. The libraries in Table 2 are the same ones we considered earlier in the chapter. These libraries allowed patrons access to tens of thousands of titles but paid nothing to give them the chance to decide whether the books were what they needed.

| Institution | PDA Titles | Number of Browses | Number of Titles Browsed | Combined List Price of Titles Browsed (USD) |
|---|---|---|---|---|
| Australian University, Victoria | 121,423 | 57,032 | 19,032 | $2,093,603 |
| US University, New Jersey | 151,237 | 9,134 | 6,022 | $582,968 |
| US University, California | 143,883 | 3,800 | 2,763 | $330,352 |

Table 2. Number of browses and overall cost of the titles browsed for books not owned by three PDA libraries. The browses cost the libraries nothing. Data are for one year, December 2009 to December 2010.

In summary, an examination period that has no financial consequences for the library is essential to a PDA program. It serves the same purpose as browsing in a bookstore, where we collect candidate titles from the shelves, then sit with our coffee and often decide to buy none of them. Without an examination period that has no financial consequences and that does not count "clicks" a PDA program is possible, but the titles to which patrons can have access will necessarily be far, far fewer.

## Simultaneous Use

It stands to reason that in a use-based program allowance for simultaneous users would be important. Requiring people to wait their turn or the library to buy several copies during the relatively brief periods when most books rise to popularity would be a money waster and would shamefully disregard the capabilities of the electronic technology.

The *when* and the *how much* of popularity are mostly impossible to predict. Books typically have a life cycle in which use of them rises to a peak and then recedes. But the rise can begin upon publication or long after publication, and the peak for a skull-crushing academic title may be a small hummock compared with the Everest of a popular novel. A book that has gone unused for years can become popular again owing to turns in world events. The astonishing appearance of a novel by the great scientist E.O. Wilson can send readers looking for copies of his old scholarly tomes, *Sociobiology* or *Consilience*. The key for a library is not to buy multiple copies during the relatively short periods when many people need one of those books at the same time.

If you consider the total career of a book in a library, then the overall time it is in use will be infinitesimal compared with the time it stands waiting. If two, five, or fifty people want one book on the same day during the long years and all but one must be turned away, then where is the sense in that? On the other hand, if the library must buy several copies to support one or a few brief shining moments of popularity, knowing that soon all of the copies will languish for years, where is the sense in that?

Paying a premium for multiple-user editions seldom makes sense. If you pay 1.5 times list price for multiple-user editions, then you get two books for the price of three. The breadth of your collection diminishes by a third. If you know that during their years of service those multiple-user editions will mostly stand and wait, then the price for a few days of simultaneous use seems exorbitant.

In summary, PDA is more than anything else a use-based concept. Because books exist in time where interest in them typically has short peaks and long valleys, the allowance for multiple-simultaneous use to accommodate the peaks, but at a price that recognizes the valleys, is prerequisite.

## Short-Term Loans

Perhaps the single most important capability in successful PDA programs is what is being called "short-term loans." A PDA program starts with books the library does *not* own. For an un-owned book, at the end of an examination period when a patron wants to continue its use, the transaction that enables the patron to keep reading will usually be a short-term loan. They work differently among the aggregators, but in general the library pays a percentage of the list price of the book so that the patron can borrow it for periods from 24 hours up to 28 days.

The value of the short-term loan comes from the pattern of use in academic libraries. Most books in a PDA program that are borrowed at all will be borrowed only a few times. As a result, rather than spend $100 to buy a book used once or twice the short-term loan makes it possible to spend $5 to $15 to allow access.

The libraries in Table 3 (different from the ones we looked at earlier) present a representative cross-section of overall budget, size, and use of short-term loans. The Michigan library allows four short-term loans and then buys a book the fifth time someone wants to check it out. The general idea is not to buy before a pattern of use emerges, and because they are much less expensive than buying, to favor short-term loans slightly over purchases. By contrast, the Connecticut library actively seeks *not to* buy, intervening before any purchase. As a result, the number of purchases compared with short-term loans is tiny.

| Institution | Number of Short-term Loans | Expenditure for Short-term Loans (USD) | Auto-Purchase X STLs | Number of Auto-Purchases | Expenditure for Auto-Purchases (USD) |
|---|---|---|---|---|---|
| US University, Michigan | 5,116 | $45,628 | 4 | 457 | $34,908 |
| US University, Connecticut | 3,218 | $23,870 | Never Without Intervention | 3 | $448 |
| Australian University, Queensland | 14,498 | $148,351 | 3 | 2,088 | $180,476 |
| Australian University, Victoria | 1,345 | $15,778 | 1 | 1,623 | $151,666 |

Table 3. Short-term loans and auto-purchases as elements of PDA programs at four libraries. Data are for one year, from December 2009 to December 2010.

The Queensland library looks for balance, but by setting the point at which it purchases one notch lower than the Michigan library (at 3 rather than 4), spends more of its budget buying than borrowing. The Victoria library strongly prefers buying to renting.

As you see, the balance of short-term loans to purchases sensitively reflects how a library wishes to spend its PDA budget. The Victoria Library favors building a collection and when patrons show interest in titles, buys them early. The Connecticut library favors access, almost never buying. Comparing these two institutions dramatically illustrates the decisive importance of short-term loans in how a PDA budget plays out.

The Connecticut library spent $24,199 on 3,221 transactions in its PDA program (STLs plus purchases). The Victoria library spent $167,444 on 2,968 transactions. If you favor collection building, the Victoria Library acquired 1,623 simultaneous-user books, the Connecticut library, three. If you favor access, the 3,218 loans for under $24,000 look like a bargain compared with 2,968 transactions for $167,444.

The Michigan and Queensland libraries, which use short-term loans and purchases slightly differently, illustrate that STLs are an economical way to allow access. For an average transaction cost of $8.92 the Michigan library can enable a patron to borrow a book through an STL; the library spends on average $76.39 to buy one. The cost of an STL for the Queensland library is $10.23; the cost of a purchase is $86.43. The ratio of loans to purchases for the Michigan library is 11:1 and for the Queensland library almost 7:1. Without STLs, the libraries could make far fewer titles visible to their patrons and could support far fewer transactions, greatly weakening the overall effectiveness of the PDA program. The STLs stretch their budgets.

## Summary

Other elements such as reasonable, consistent copying and printing allowances and the ability to download to computers or reading devices are useful in a PDA program. But these features should be characteristics of ebooks under any circumstances and are not specific elements of PDA. The examination period, reasonably priced simultaneous use, and short-term loans are essential.

### A Model for Planning and Targeting a PDA Program

Because PDA is new and because old incarnations of it led to expensive failures, libraries have assumed that it is unpredictable. One result has been experiment after careful experiment, the tendency to approach it with interest but extreme caution. Libraries have assumed that PDA is so unruly that about all they can do is put a finger in the wind and hope for the best when budgeting,

In fact, however, a strategically deployed PDA program rolled out conservatively and monitored from its beginning is malleable and predictable to within 5 percent – and often 1 percent – of the budget a library has in mind. In the final section of this chapter, I will lay out a model of budgeting for PDA at academic libraries that support fewer than 20,000 and more than 20,000 patrons. The model complements Dennis Dillon's in the preceding chapter. Where Dennis describes the careful budget process the University of Texas at Austin uses, I look across a database that goes back to 2004 and that includes dozens of libraries. Where Dennis is a practitioner generalizing from particular experience, I am writing as a supplier using aggregated data to create a formula that works for specific libraries. On the other hand, where I write from the point of view of one specific aggregator, Dennis works with all of them. Together our points of view should prove a good primer for anyone ready to try a PDA program.

Based on data collected beginning in 2004 we have used dozens of successful PDA programs from large and small libraries worldwide as the basis for the model that follows. The data are prolific, consistent over time, and emerge from many circumstances.

## Elements of the PDA Model

Building a PDA program requires understanding the interaction of the following variables:

1. A budget.
2. The purchase trigger.
3. Number of patrons who use the library or who can be expected to use the books in the PDA program.
4. Number of titles to which the patrons have access.

Designing a PDA program based on the interaction of these factors is straightforward and makes the workflow predictable.

In general you begin with a budget. With that understood, we talk about the purchase trigger, whether the library prefers to own or to rent, and at what point buying makes sense. The number of patrons is clear enough, but not always a given. If a PDA program will cover only certain subjects, then the number of students and faculty involved with those programs, rather than the overall population the library supports, is what matters. With these characteristics understood, we aim to begin with a conservative number of titles that the budget will certainly support. The backbone of a PDA program usually is a list of already published titles that fit criteria the library lays out. If the list is too small, the budget will not be spent. We are careful to begin with a list that is not too large. And finally, most libraries create a profile that adds new books as they are published or become part of the canon of titles available from the aggregator.

Once the PDA program begins we watch it closely for the first weeks and months. Libraries themselves can look at up-to-the-minute online invoices for STLs and for auto-purchases. Patterns take shape quickly, and after three months we have enough data to project expenditures. Usually, because the start is conservative by design, a library can add more titles to the program at the end of the first quarter, but it is always possible to withdraw titles and to change settings, such as the number of uses that triggers a purchase or the amount at which an STL or a purchase will be mediated. In other words, various controls on the rate of expenditure and tools for seeing exactly where the program stands make it easily manageable, not mysterious or surprising.

## Targeting PDA

As we saw earlier, some libraries use PDA programs almost entirely as a means to provide access, preferring to buy books rarely. Most libraries, however, see building a collection through owning books as an important function. For those libraries, PDA introduces *use* as a new variable. That is, for the part of the collection built through a PDA workflow, rather than buy based on a profile that defines what is appropriate for the library to own, *use* becomes the main criterion for purchase. The profile still applies, but at first books that fit simply live unowned in the catalogue. The gauntlet through which they pass into ownership is composed of the number of short-term loans – 1, 2,3, or more – a library applies. As we have seen (Table 3), short-term loans are a sensitive trigger for establishing purchasing practices. Where libraries emphasize ownership – but use-based ownership – the number of STLs that occur before a purchase is set low, at one or two loans.

In working out the model, we[2] examined 35 colleges and universities in Australia, Canada, New Zealand, and the United States. Of these, 25 had full-blown, well established PDA programs and 7 had either outright purchase programs or attenuated PDA programs. The remaining institutions were in relatively early stages of establishing PDA.

The sections that follow look at institutions that serve fewer than 20,000 and more than 20,000. Importantly, in creating a PDA program we would look more closely at the number of patrons a library supports and would consider other factors beyond the scope of the general model presented here. For example, a college built mainly to support distance learning would see more relative activity in a PDA program than a

---

2   Robin Champieux of EBL gathered data, organized our thinking, and helped reach the conclusions presented here.

traditional campus. The model that follows describes how to build PDA programs that emphasize access, emphasize use-based collection building, or balance the two.

## Building the Model

An Australian university with an FTE of nearly 40,000 students and a Massachusetts college of fewer than 3,000 included about 40,000 titles in their PDA programs from December 2009 through December 2010. Both offered one-day and one-week short-term loans.[3] The Australian university spent $165,857 to support its demand-driven program, compared with $25,568 for the college. The dramatic difference comes from use patterns occasioned by the size of each.

At the college, patrons browsed 5.5 percent of the total PDA titles and triggered short-term loans for 2.4 percent of them. At the University, patrons browsed 29 percent of the list and triggered short-term loans for 14 percent of its titles. Ultimately, the college purchased fewer than 1 percent of the PDA titles, the university 8.4 percent. Perhaps most interesting is that the pattern for the college holds generally for institutions under 20,000, and the university's pattern typically applies for institutions over 20,000. Finally, both programs demonstrated a similar value. To allow access to 40,000 titles, the college paid 17.4% of the list price of the titles its users browsed (remember, they browsed 5.5 percent of the 40,000) and borrowed; the university paid 16% of the total list price of the titles its patrons browsed (29 percent of the 40,000) and borrowed. In other words the correlation between titles in the program, patrons who have access to them, and overall expenditure are strongly predictable at small and large institutions.

---

3   With some aggregators the library sets the length of a short-term loan. The longer the loan, the more it costs. Many libraries allow their patrons to choose the length of some loans. When they do, then the average cost of STLs rises overall because many times patrons select the longer, more expensive loan. The overall effect of longer loans on a PDA program is discernible but relatively minor.

## Building a PDA Program for Libraries that Support Fewer than 20,000 Patrons

Libraries at institutions that support fewer than 20,000 patrons must buy books very selectively, which widens the gap between what patrons need and what the library is likely to own. PDA can have the dramatic immediate effect of making a library look much bigger than it could hope to be if forced to buy every book it offered. As a result, libraries at small and mid-sized institutions are likely to use PDA more as a tool for access than as a means of use-based purchasing, are likely to emphasize borrowing over buying.

The statistical probabilities inherent in PDA support this direction. As we saw above, libraries at very small institutions can make the same number, or more, titles available for much less money than a larger institution could make them available. When 3,000 or fewer patrons are searching a catalogue that includes 150,000 PDA titles, they will find, browse, borrow, and ultimately buy far fewer than if 40,000 patrons are searching the catalogue. Approval plans were often said to be tools for big libraries. PDA plans work well for small and mid-sized ones.

We have discussed several of the libraries in Table 4, but collectively they make several points about programs that support 20,000 or fewer patrons. Most important, the overall budget for a full-blown PDA program that has significant effect need not exceed $25,000 and can be less at smaller institutions. Conversely, the largest budgets support tens of thousands of titles and thousands of transactions.

In Table 4, the effects of the interaction among number of titles in the program, the auto-purchase point, and the number of patrons supported are in almost lockstep. Here, the smallest institutions (the two under 3,000) purchase early, after 1 and 2 STLs; as a result they spend more on purchases than the other institutions of 5,000 or fewer despite their smaller base of patrons. The library from Victoria also buys after two STLs, spends more on purchasing than on renting, and spends more on purchasing than any other library in the Table. The result of emphasizing purchases is fewer transactions for their budgets than libraries that favor STLs.

| Institution | PDA Titles | Auto-purchase after X STLs | Patrons | STL Expenses (USD) | STLs (No.) | Auto-purchases (USD) | Auto-purchases (No.) |
|---|---|---|---|---|---|---|---|
| Canada, Nova Scotia | 122,657 | 1 | 2,787 | $9,294 | 908 | $21,963 | 258 |
| US, Massachusetts | 41,203 | 2 | 2,324 | $14,882 | 1175 | $9,687 | 110 |
| US, Connecticut | 139,848 | Never without manual intervention | 5,074 | $23,870 | 3218 | $329 | 3 |
| US, California | 143,883 | 3 | 3,414 | $28,399 | 1888 | $2,632 | 34 |
| US, Pennsylvania | 44,898 | 3 | 3,953 | $17,738 | 1401 | $4,417 | 38 |
| Australia, New South Wales | 148,106 | 3 | 17,817 | $69,612 | 7,498 | $43,826 | 428 |
| US, New Jersey | 151,237 | 3 | 15,051 | $30,791 | 3,521 | $9,257 | 125 |
| Australia, Victoria | 145,587 | 2 | 12,888 | $55,015 | 5,462 | $72,425 | 726 |
| US, Alaska | 114,237 | 3 | 9,137 | $41,898 | 4,098 | $16,019 | 156 |

Table 4. Budgeting for PDA in academic libraries that serve fewer than 20,000 patrons. Data are for one year from December 2009 to December 2010.

Conversely, the most purchase-averse library in the group, the one from Connecticut, spends less on purchases and less overall than any other, has a large number of titles in the program, and has more transactions per dollar because it almost never buys a book.

When libraries support 5,000 patrons or fewer, the setting for the number of loans that triggers a purchase has an outsized effect on the disposition of the budget. The cost of STLs usually averages from $8 to $10; the cost of purchases averages from $75 to $100. In a small program, a few purchases are quickly felt against the overall budget. If the library favors buying and so keeps the number of loans before purchase low, the high cost of buying compared with renting accumulates quickly as a percentage of the budget. As a result, the total transactions possible within the PDA framework diminishes accordingly. On the other hand, the number of titles in the PDA program is a less significant variable for libraries at small schools than for libraries at large ones. Adding 10,000 titles increases costs only slightly at a small institution because few will ever be found, fewer browsed, and a (relatively) small subset loaned or bought.

If colleges and universities of 5,000 or fewer can have a strong PDA program for $25,000 or even less, $40,000 to $125,000 usually is suitable for libraries that support 10,000 to 20,000 patrons. Lower budgets typically coincide with a program meant for fewer purchases, higher budgets for more. The thing we do not see in Table 4 for the libraries that support more than 10,000 patrons is an example that radically favors renting to purchasing. Only now are libraries beginning to try five, six, or seven STLs before they purchase. For a mid-sized library that wishes to include a high number of titles in its PDA program, the STL strategy will prove effective.

## Universities of More than 20,000

At about 20,000 patrons a tipping point occurs. Above all, the number of titles in the PDA program – the "risk pool" as Dennis Dillon calls it – becomes especially consequential, and beyond 30,000 it bears close watching. The libraries in Table 5 with above 30,000 patrons all have fewer than 100,000 PDA titles despite significant budgets. The thing to think hardest about for these libraries is the number of transactions that their budgets allow.

| Institution | PDA Titles | Auto-purchase after X STLs | Patrons | STL Expenses (USD) | STLs (No.) | Auto-purchase (USD) | Auto-purchase (No.) |
|---|---|---|---|---|---|---|---|
| US, Texas | 80,861 | 3 | 50,000+ | $170,564 | 17,597 | $226,396 | 2,555 |
| Australia, Queensland | 76,260 | 3 | 40,000+ | $148,351 | 14,498 | $180,476 | 2,088 |
| Australia, Victoria (1) | 40,709 | 3 | 36,814 | $81,775 | 8,623 | $84,083 | 993 |
| US, Michigan | 135,566 | 4 | 24,408 | $45,628 | 5,116 | $34,908 | 457 |
| Canada, Ontario | 55,183 | 3 | 23,558 | $47,725 | 3,177 | $26,270 | 303 |
| Australia, Victoria (2) | 121,423 | 3 | 22,046 | $94,596 | 9,260 | $106,659 | 1,121 |
| Australia, Victoria (3) | 145,141 | 3 | 22,500 | $296,950 | 24,581 | $201,670 | 1,790 |

Table 5. Trends in PDA programs at libraries that support more than 20,000 patrons. Data are for one year from December 2009 to December 2010.

The three largest libraries exemplify the effect of number of titles in the PDA program, and the effect of the auto-purchase point on the disposition of the budget. The Texas library has the largest budget and the most titles; the Queensland and Victoria (1) libraries have fewer titles and smaller budgets. Each of the three sets its auto-purchase after 3 STLs and as a result, each spends slightly more on auto-purchases than on STLs.

The libraries that support fewer than 30,000 patrons can include more titles in their PDA programs for less money. A good example of how this works appears in Table 6. For the three largest libraries, about 30 percent of the PDA titles available are accessed. For the libraries that support fewer than 30,000 patrons the percent drops to a high of 21 and to as low as 5 percent at the Michigan library. Each library has factors outside the PDA program that influence the extent to which titles in the program are used. The size of the overall collection and the number of ebooks the library owns or to which it subscribes are important. But clearly, more patrons mean more of the PDA titles will be discovered and used. The rate of use for libraries above 20,000 is predictable enough that with a budget in mind and a conservative number of PDA titles to start, a library can confidently take advantage of the benefits of a PDA program.

| Institution | PDA Titles | Patrons | Percent of PDA Titles Accessed |
|---|---|---|---|
| US, Texas | 80,861 | 50,000+ | 32.84 |
| Australia, Queensland | 76,260 | 40,000+ | 28.80 |
| Australia, Victoria (2) | 40,709 | 36,814 | 29.10 |
| US, Michigan | 135,566 | 24,408 | 5.22 |
| Canada, Ontario | 55,183 | 23,558 | 16.52 |
| Australia, Victoria | 121,423 | 22,046 | 15.67 |
| Australia, Victoria (3) | 145,141 | 22,500 | 21.02 |

Table 6. Correlation between titles visible, patrons served, and titles accessed among universities serving more than 20,000 patrons

## Conclusion

At my (advanced) age, getting through a hard chapter full of (ugh) Tables is bad enough. Remembering anything that it said is probably impossible. That is, thank you for the effort, and if nothing stuck, do not worry. In the interest of rewarding anyone brave or committed enough to have traveled this far, I will be brief and simple. The lessons of this chapter are:

1. A PDA program is not alchemy. Better than that, its chief outcomes, access or collection building, are easily balanced or one or the other emphasized. Best of all, a PDA program that has measurable effects for the library can be undertaken on a small budget and scaled up only as it proves its worth.
2. Of the characteristics that a PDA model might have, so far the most important are an examination period, reasonably priced simultaneous use, and short-term loans.
3. If you embark on a PDA program, old ideas about how to manage monographs will impose themselves on your thinking. Overcoming them to at least some degree will give your program more scope and more value.

## Reference

Hodges, Dracine, Cyndi Preston, and Marsha J. Hamilton. "Patron-Initiated Collection Development: Progress of a Paradigm Shift." *Collection Management* 35 (2010): 208-221.

# Part 4
# Conclusion

# Chapter 12
# PDA and Libraries Today and Tomorrow

Dennis Dillon

*University of Texas, Austin*

Today, librarians live in a world in which more information is available outside the library than inside. The library is no longer the only doorway to scarce information; instead, it is one information room in a very large house that is overflowing with information. Too many information options exist for any one person to discover or for one library to house. This is particularly true with ebooks, where consumers are driving the ebook revolution and libraries are being left by the wayside. Consumers, for example, have access to millions of ebooks that are not being sold to libraries. Consumers can go to Amazon or to Google ebooks and download titles to a device within a few seconds, at any hour of the day or night. The new consumer utopia of instantly available digital books is leaving the library behind as a relic of a bygone age when users were not self-sufficient and when the information or book a user wanted was not simply a click away. In Google's case, these books will soon be available for sale in every major language on earth. Before long more books will be for sale to consumers than currently exist in even the largest library, and the books will live in the worldwide computing cloud where they can be downloaded to almost any device, at any time, for the rest of the consumer's life. In this environment librarians have to think more systematically and more creatively. Demand-driven acquisition can be part of the answer.

Demand-driven acquisition frees librarians from the time-consuming process of making thousands of small, routine, item-by-item decisions, and allows them to elevate their sights so that they can make more significant, more professional contributions that have a wider effect on what information their users can access. Demand-driven acquisition allows libraries to compete, at least on a small scale, with behemoths like Google and Amazon, with their millions of cheap downloadable books. Demand-driven acquisition has the potential to make the librarian a professional content manager who no longer spends hours every week making $50 decisions, and instead makes $50,000 decisions, using his or her freed-up time to work on improving access, discovery, and the library's relevancy.

Librarians who work in a world of easily available ebooks will need to become comfortable with the idea of the self-sufficient user who may never set foot in the library, never ask questions, never call, never send e-mail, and never use chat, but who reads ebooks and uses the other online content, and who also has the power to easily obtain books from non-library sources within seconds. In this world librarians need to have information strategies that can at least approach the information nimbleness of the consumer. Demand-driven acquisition allows libraries to leverage their money to the fullest by offering tens of thousands, even hundreds of thousands of ebooks to their users, even though today's large library may realistically expect to eventually purchase and own only 10 to 15 percent of this content and a small library even less.

Libraries may never be able to replicate the impact an individual librarian had on an individual customer back in that pre-digital, print-focused era when obscurity and uncertainty were the bibliographic rule, and when painfully gained specialized knowledge was a necessity for any librarian to be effective. But every librarian can still make a difference in the lives of their customers, and can still influence the publishers and vendors with whom they interact by working to make more ebooks available to libraries through an increasing number of different business models. It is important to emphasize that if demand-driven acquisition is to have a future both the library and the publisher must be comfortable with the models that trigger a demand-driven charge. In demand-driven scenarios, both the publisher and the library share risk. The risk for the library is that ebooks will prove so useful to patrons that the library will quickly exhaust its funds. The risk for the publisher is that few will want to read their books and that they will collect little revenue for their investment. The obvious incentive for the publisher is to publish books that users want to read; for the library the incentive is to allocate adequate funds so that readers have access to the books they want.

## Issues: Ebook Formats, DRM, Downloading, Printing, Mobile Devices and Consumer Technologies

Today's ebooks still have significant ease-of-use issues. Consumer technology keeps moving ahead, and users demand that the ebooks they personally purchase be usable in the ways they want. Ebooks sold to libraries are not under these same pressures because the library market is much smaller and because some publishers fear that every ebook sold to a library means lost consumer sales. As a result, consumer friendly features have been slower to emerge in the library market. These issues will be solved and are almost entirely caused by overly cumbersome digital rights management software that is designed to control and limit who and how each ebook file is used. Since demand-driven programs work best with digital data that can be delivered instantaneously at the point of need to a multitude of devices, lessening digital rights management restrictions will be critical to future success, as will the ability to interact with and allow downloading to the growing multitude of mobile devices.

## Who is the Collection For?

Demand-driven acquisition occasionally revives old questions about who the library collection is for. Is it for users or for librarians? Is it for current users, or is it a record of civilization for the next generation? The best response to anyone concerned at the idea of users selecting library content is the obvious one: the library is for everyone. Professional librarians can continue to select part of the content, and nowadays users can also help by selecting a portion. Demand-driven acquisition gives users a more active say in their library collection. And a collection that is the result of librarian-reader collaboration will be stronger than a collection built solely on a librarian's speculative purchases, which are no more than educated guesses about what readers might someday need. In the years we have been doing demand-driven selection, users have consistently chosen high-quality books and have helped to diversify the collection. In many cases, user selections have, not surprisingly, been ahead of the librarian selections because the users are the ones doing the research, working in the labs, conducting the fieldwork, and studying the latest disciplinary trends. Simply put, individual readers know what is in their own interest better than librarians do. In the past the librarian's only options were to resort to speculation, suggestion boxes, and mental telepathy if we were going to determine what our readers wanted. Now librarians have a new tool in their arsenal.

## The Future

At a time when library budgets are under stress and when technological changes continue to expand the universe of content available to consumers, library effectiveness and funding depend on being responsive to users' needs. They depend on being able to carve a niche that allows libraries to compete against the offerings and instant gratification of iTunes, Amazon, Netflix, Google ebooks, and whatever happens to be the latest flavor in disruptive Web information products. Libraries no longer have the luxury of wasting scarce funds on services and content that are unneeded or seldom used. Demand-driven acquisition is arguably the single best way to leverage the funds that libraries have, and it gives libraries a new tool to compete in an era of widespread instant ebook access. Demand-driven acquisition also forces libraries to understand their users at a level that libraries have never had to consider before, because they require libraries to prepare bottom-line budgets based on the realities of their users' actual behavior.

Looking ahead, demand-driven acquisition can be expected to develop many new business modes and options as publishers, vendors, and librarians gain more experience with what works for all parties. We can expect vendors to introduce business models that produce revenue from both larger and smaller pieces of content than in the past and from specific actions, such as micropayments for saving or printing a single page, or small subscription charges for those libraries that maintain records for more than a million demand-driven titles. Demand-driven acquisition is a new way of splitting the financial risk between the library, the information vendor, and the content producer. The risk can be split in many ways. Traditionally the publisher took on considerable risk in producing content that might or might not sell, and libraries took on risk by buying books that might not be used. Modern academic libraries have been structured through the use of approval plans over the past forty years to provide a predictable revenue source for academic publishers, but financial problems and technology are changing this once stolid equation.

What does demand-driven workflow mean for librarians? It means letting go of comfortable patterns of thought. It means becoming comfortable with less control, with less ownership, and with being surprised at the previously unknown interests of our users. It means entertaining the idea that there are better ways of doing things. It means recognizing that many library users have skills and knowledge that can help the library navigate rapidly shifting financial and consumer realities. It means being willing to confront the uncomfortable reality that the clock is ticking on the utility of traditional library approaches, and that libraries are in a competitive situation in which our greatest strength may be our ability to partner with and trust the library user.

# About the Authors

*Ron Berry – Associate Director for Library and Academic Technology at New York University – Abu Dhabi.* Before returning to the Middle East Berry was the Associate Dean for Technology and Information Resources at Grand Valley State University in Michigan. He holds an MLS from the University of British Columbia. Ron continues has long been interested in challenging assumptions of library services and finding solutions.

*Thomas B. Corbett – Executive Director, Fisher-Watkins Library, Cushing Academy.* Corbett has overseen the controversial transformation of Cushing Academy's library away from print and toward a primarily digital collection, while still remaining deeply committed to monographs and other long-form reading. As the first U.S. high school to fully adopt a PDA approach to collection development, Cushing Academy has been a leader in finding ways to make a secondary school library relevant, and even vibrant, in the 21st Century. Corbett holds an MLS from the University of Missouri.

*Emilie Delquié is Vice-President of Publishers Communication Group* and has been an active member of the information industry for more than eleven years. She joined PCG, a sales and marketing consulting firm, in 2005, after working for five years with the collection development team at the University of Massachusetts-Boston Library. She is now working closely with over 100 publishers to implement marketing campaigns designed to increase customer retention and grow institutional subscriptions. Recently, she has been conducting studies on librarians' attitudes toward ebooks and patron-driven acquisition.

*Dennis Dillon – Associate Director for Research Services at The University Libraries of The University of Texas at Austin.* He is also the long-time administrator for the University of Texas System's Academic Library Collection Enhancement Program, which purchases shared library resources on behalf of the System's fifteen institutions. He has purchased several hundred thousand dollars worth of ebooks annually since 1999, with Texas ebook acquisitions exceeding $1 million in recent years. He is a frequent writer and speaker on ebooks and the future of libraries.

*Julie Garrison* is the *Associate Dean for Research and Instructional Services at Grand Valley State University*, where she has been since February 2007. Before this Julie was the Director of Off-Campus Library Services at Central Michigan University and Associate Director of Public Services at Duke University Medical Center Library. Julie holds an MLIS degree from UCLA and started her library career when the Web was in its infancy. She has written and presented on many collections and distance-education topics. Julie dances a stormy polka.

*Michael Levine-Clark* is the *Collections Librarian at the University of Denver's Penrose Library* and has also held positions as a reference and documents librarian. He has an MS in Library and Information Science from the University of Illinois, and an MA in History from the University of Iowa. With colleagues from the Colorado Alliance of Research Libraries, he founded the open access journal *Collaborative Librarianship*, and he serves as co-editor for scholarly articles. He has published and presented widely on various aspects of collections use and analysis, and is especially interested in how these analyses can inform practice.

*Rick Lugg is partner in R2 Consulting LLC*, a practice focused on academic library strategies and workflows and *President of Sustainable Collections LLC*, which provides tools for data-driven de-selection of monographs. He holds an MLS from Simmons College. Rick is a native of New Hampshire, whose official motto "Live Free or Die" and unofficial secondary motto "Common Sense for All" have shaped his worldview.

*Bob Nardini is Vice President, Product Development at Coutts Information Services*, a division of the Ingram Content Group. He worked in both public and academic libraries until 1985, before taking a job in the academic bookselling industry, where he has been ever since. In 2007 Nardini joined Coutts and is involved in several areas of the company's activity, especially development of the OASIS customer interface and MyiLibrary ebook platform, approval plan services development, and sales and marketing. Nardini writes a column in *Against the Grain* and holds an M.A. in History from the University of Virginia and an M.L.S. from the University of Toronto. He lives in Nashville, Tennessee and Chichester, New Hampshire.

*Kari Paulson* is the *President and founder of Ebook Library (EBL),* a subsidiary of Ebooks Corporation and has more than a decade of experience with ebook technology. Growing up in Minnesota, Kari was drawn to winter sports and began her career as a professional figure skater in Europe. She has been a voice agent, a radio producer, a production manager for a film producer, and project manager for a web development company. A dual American and Australian citizen, Kari now lives in London.

*Sue Polanka – Head of Reference and Instruction at the Wright State University Libraries in Dayton, Ohio.* Polanka is the moderator of the award-winning, No Shelf Required®, a blog about the issues surrounding ebooks for librarians and publishers. She has been a reference and instruction librarian for over 20 years at public, state, and academic libraries in Ohio and Texas. She edited, *No Shelf Required: E-books in Libraries*, from ALA Editions; is currently editing *E-Reference Context and Discoverability in Libraries: Issues and Concepts* with IGI Publishing; and *No Shelf Required II: The Use and Management of E-Books*. She was on Booklist's Reference Books Bulletin Editorial Board for over ten years, serving as Chair from 2007 through 2010. Her column on electronic reference, *Off The Shelf*, appears in *Booklist*, quarterly. Polanka was named a 2011 *Library Journal* Mover and Shaker.

*Rex Steiner – Library Director, Azerbaijan Diplomatic Academy, Baku, Azerbaijan.* Steiner has spent almost 15-years dealing with or working in international academic and special libraries. He has had a hand in the planning, operating, or opening of eight international libraries in that time, mostly in the Arabian Gulf. The American University of Sharjah, the Petroleum Institute in Abu Dhabi, and most recently the Azerbaijan Diplomatic Academy are all institutions where Rex has had a leadership role. He has an MLS from Emporia State University.

*David A. Swords – Vice President, Sales and Marketing, Ebook Library (EBL)*
Before coming to EBL in January 2010, Swords was head of Sales and Marketing for Blackwell and before that was Vice President of International Sales for YBP Library Services. He taught technical writing for many years at the University of New Orleans and now lives in New Hampshire. The idea for this book came from a chance meeting with

Alice Keller, now an editor with Walter de Gruyter and formerly of the Bodleian Library, at ALA in summer 2010.

*Doug Way – Head of Collections at Grand Valley State University* where he previously served as Head of Liberal Arts Programs and Government Documents Librarian. Doug has written and presented extensively in the areas of library collection management, the use of library collections, and scholarly communications.

# Index